The Professional Contract Worker's Yearbook

To Luke,

Multimedia
   Designer

Love Im

H7 lr .

X X X X X

THE PROFESSIONAL CONTRACT WORKER'S YEARBOOK

1996 Edition

HELEN GEORGE

THE McGRAW-HILL COMPANIES

London · New York · St Louis · San Francisco · Auckland
Bogotá · Caracas · Lisbon · Madrid · Mexico
Milan · Montreal · New Delhi · Panama · Paris · San Juan
São Paulo · Singapore · Sydney · Tokyo · Toronto

Published by McGraw-Hill Publishing Company
Shoppenhangers Road, Maidenhead, Berkshire, SL6 2QL,
England
Telephone 01628 23432
Fax 01628 770224

British Library Cataloguing in Publication Data
George, Helen
  The professional contract worker's handbook
  1.Temporary employment 2.Labour contract 3.Self-employed
  I.Title
  331.1'25

  ISBN 0–07–709314–3

Library of Congress Cataloging-in-Publication Data
The CIP data of this title is available from the Library of
Congress, Washington DC, USA

McGraw-Hill

*A Division of The **McGraw·Hill** Companies*

12345 CL 99876

Typeset by Ian Kingston Editorial Services, Nottingham
Printed in Great Britain at the University Press, Cambridge

Printed on permanent paper in compliance with ISO Standard
9706

Contents

Preface

In a way, I am surprised that I have ended up writing this book – surprised that no one has done it before me. When I started contract-working, eight years ago, I went up and down the High Street book stores trying to find a book about professional contract-working. There were plenty of books about running small businesses or being a consultant or being self-employed. I read half a dozen of them and gradually pieced together some of what I needed to know. But none of them even mentioned contract work, and they were all rather impersonal.

Time passed; I continued contract-working and clocked up the usual number of expensive or time-consuming mistakes while I learned the ropes. The contract market, meanwhile, was expanding rapidly. More and more of my friends, in all kinds of professional fields, decided to take to contract-working. They would ask me various questions about setting up as a contractor and I would tell them what I knew and what the main problems about setting up as a contractor were. And then they would always say, 'What I need is a book to read all this up in'. And I would say, 'Well, by now there probably is one'. And again and again I would be told that there was no book available. And that is how I came to write *The Professional Contract Worker's Yearbook*.

I do not claim to know everything that there is to know about contract-working, and like most contractors I owe an awful lot to the contractors I have worked with over the years, who have been extremely generous with advice and information. In part that is because contractors have to help each other. The government, the media and the Civil Service have been very slow to catch on to this new way of working. So contractors have developed a kind of pioneering spirit. They know they are not going to get much help from published sources or officialdom, so they help each other. Contractors frequently have to set up their own companies, run their own accounts, market themselves, take their own precautions against sickness, train themselves, make their own provisions for retirement – it is no wonder that many contractors consider themselves totally self-sufficient.

I hope *The Professional Contract Worker's Yearbook* can be both a useful reference book and a summary of some of the issues that concern contractors. Some of these change constantly; some (such as travelling expenses) seem to simmer on year after year. Next year's edition will be bigger, and with your help will have information from contractors and agencies across the whole range of industries.

As contractors we are the ones who know what 'The New Work' really is and how it affects our lives and our attitudes – we do not need management gurus, government 'think tanks', newspaper pundits or doom-ridden TV documentaries to tell us about The New Work – we are already doing it or thinking seriously about moving over to it.

This book is for all of you who are not scared of the future but would perhaps like a little more information to help you on your way. Good luck and good contracts in 1996!

PS! If you have a spare ten minutes, use the Contractor's Comment Form at the back of the book and make your voice heard.

Disclaimer

Financial and business advice and opinions in this book are general. No reader should take financial or business decisions without first taking independent professional advice which takes full account of their personal circumstances. Neither McGraw-Hill nor the author accept responsibility for decisions based on material in *The Professional Contract Worker's Yearbook*.

PART 1

A New Way of Working

1 The New Work

This book is the key resource for a new breed of worker – the contractor. As the 1990s progress, more and more professionals are moving over to contract work or developing 'portfolio' careers. This book tells you what's going on and gives you the extra knowledge you need to become a successful contractor. It also includes a 'look-up' section (Part 4) which gives specific information on contract work across a wide range of industries.

It is true of many things (the Internet being a prime example) that they only get reported once they start affecting journalists. So it is with contract work. As the kinds of practice that encourage companies to use contract workers spread into broadcasting and media organizations, affecting journalists' and programme makers' jobs we are beginning to see articles and documentaries expressing grave concern at this new trend. The tone of these articles tells us more about journalists' worries than it does about the true nature of contract work, but we can expect to see many more in the years to come, because the one thing you can say for sure about contract work is that, in every sector, it is growing.

Which Industries use Contractors?

The truth is – all of them, sooner or later. For example, the contract market for IT workers has existed for 30 or more years and is highly developed. But contract work is now established right across industry, government, health, social services and business.

It is worth noting in this context that the rising figures for workers in self-employment do not accurately reflect the rising numbers of contract workers. This is because of an obscure clause in the Taxes Act which means that many agencies will only give contracts to people who are trading as limited companies. Although the limited company has only one employee – the contractor – this person is counted as employed rather than self-employed. The issue of how you trade as a contractor is a large one and we shall look at it in detail in Chapter 5.

Why do Organizations use Contract Workers?

We are all aware that organizations shed jobs throughout the recession of the early 1990s. But all those redundancies were an expensive exercise for the organizations and companies involved. As a patchy recovery gets under way, many want to undertake a modest expansion or carry out capital spending on projects. Yet they do not want to increase the head-count of permanent staff, especially when no one is certain for how long staff will be needed. Most companies want to cut their fixed costs, and staff are usually a large part of those costs. The obvious answer is to take on contract staff to cover extra workload, who can be shed as soon as the extra work has been completed. Alternatively, if the need for extra staff is proved, the position can be advertised and filled by a permanent employee.

*Increase in
Project Work*

The use of contract workers fits particularly well with project work. And another reason for the growth in demand for contract workers is, quite simply, a growth in the number of projects. Companies are tending to view development in terms of projects and to assemble teams to achieve the project goals. This is an ideal scenario for contract workers because organizations seeking to fill project roles have very specific ideas about the kind of individuals they are looking for.

At the same time, highly skilled people are becoming increasingly expensive. Throughout Europe and the USA, marketable skills are at a premium and the salary differential between highly skilled and unskilled workers is growing rapidly.

This trend reinforces the internal dynamics of the contract market. If you are going to have to pay a lot to get the skills you want, then every other employee benefit – holidays, sick pay, pension provision, car – is going to be correspondingly expensive. So one way to control costs is to buy the person's labour only. It may be more expensive in the short term, but there's no increase in head-count and no long-term commitment beyond the immediate project financing.

*Quantifiable
Costs*

One of the other things companies like about employing contractors is that it makes it possible to plan project finance more accurately. They know to within £100 per week what a contractor will cost; there will be no sick leave, training, holiday pay or other add-on costs.

Ready-trained People

Another impetus towards this 'outsourcing' is that companies have come to realize that in an increasingly competitive, global and technology-driven world, it is pointless to try to keep expertise in every area in-house. It is better to buy in real experts when needed than it is to keep not-very-expert people on the payroll. And using contractors means that a major expense – training – can be discounted. Contractors are responsible for their own training, and they factor the costs of this into their hourly or daily rate. But since they arrive ready-trained, the employer is still probably in pocket. After all, in many organizations, if permanent staff members are sent for training, their jobs have to be covered by others, which adds to the costs.

Business Process Re-engineering

A similar pressure has been exerted by business process re-engineering. This involves taking a radical look at what a business is actually trying to do and redesigning its business processes from the ground up. In part, BPR is a response to a growing realization that previous implementations of technology, or organizational changes, simply automated or reorganized an underlying inefficiency. Why has this meant more emphasis on the contract market? Simply because BPR is a very effective way of sorting out a company's core activities from those that are necessary but peripheral. The company can then keep staff to carry out its core activities and use contractors to accomplish peripheral tasks on a project-by-project basis.

An End to Paternalism

It also has to be said that the move towards using contractors has at least coincided with, if not been prompted by, a revolution in corporate and organizational attitudes towards employees.

The former paternalistic attitude of employers, in which communal, social benefits (the staff restaurant, social club and nursery) provided a kind of add-on social wage, is vanishing. Employers do not see themselves in a parental role towards their employees. The contract between employer and employee is becoming redefined as a purely commercial one, in which employees are paid to exercise their skills but must then make their own private provision for their other needs, including vocational training.

The contract ethos fits well with this new culture, and in fact takes it to its ultimate expression. In the contract relationship, the employer has no obligations whatsoever to the worker. It is purely a business transaction. What has changed, however, is the power of skilled, ready-trained workers to extract a high cash price as their side of this bargain. The labour market, as we shall see later, works both ways.

'Just in Time'
Procedures

'Just in time' procedures have also had a large influence on the way companies see human resources. 'Just in time' procedures are a way of making industrial production more efficient by delivering the right quantity of materials into the production process at the right place and only when they are actually needed. That way expensive capital is not tied up in warehoused raw material or stockpiled finished goods. You can think of many organizations' attitudes to the contract market as a labour market application of this principle. People are used only when needed, and then they are used to full capacity.

What's the Difference Between a Contractor and a Freelance?

In general, freelances work directly for their clients. They don't usually sign a contract for each piece of work; written confirmation and a purchase order number are usually sufficient basis for an agreement and frequently the agreement is purely verbal. In general, contractors don't work directly for an organization; their contract is with an agency which in turn has a contract with the client. However, there are exceptions to this rule, particularly in the media, where production companies act in a kind of intermediary role between client and contractor, and agencies are less common.

How does the Contract Market Work?

In most industries with developed contract marketplaces, agencies have sprung up to help contractors and employers make contact. In industries where contract work is a new phenomenon there may be few agencies, a situation which will change as contractors realize there is a market opportunity and set up new agencies to capitalize on their industry contacts. In developed contract markets, such as the IT market, there are hundreds of agencies engaged in intense competition on two fronts: they have to compete for both contracts and contractors.

Clearly the general economic climate is a factor here. Contract markets are highly responsive to trading conditions. In a time of recession agencies find that contracts are scarce but contractors are not. Pay levels for contractors respond almost immediately – if a contractor has been waiting four weeks for a contract, he or she is well aware of the state of the market and knows that the best course of action is to accept a contract and not fuss too much about the money. Clients can squeeze maximum value from agencies in these circumstances, so that agencies themselves may have to cut their margins in order to offer good value to the client while paying out the market rate to the contractor.

It is in these circumstances that Preferred Supplier Agreements (discussed in Chapter 2) often come into force, as another means for the employing company (the agency's client) to control costs.

For Every Downturn, an Upturn

But when recession lifts, the scenario neatly reverses itself. There are two golden words guaranteed to make contractors rub their hands with glee: *skills shortage*. Skills shortages may worry governments and vex employers but it's an ill wind that blows nobody any good – and for highly skilled contractors skill shortages are an excellent thing.

As for the agencies, they now find contracts easy to get but their problem is reversed – contractors are hard to get. Again, contractors know way ahead of the Treasury when the market is picking up. Instead of waiting for work when they finish a contract, they receive half a dozen calls a week from agencies asking when they are available. Contractors immediately up the going rate, knowing that if one agency declines, there are lots of other contracts going. (In the USA, the government actually surveys the contract employment market to get early information on economic trends.)

In these circumstances, Preferred Supplier Agreements tend to weaken because the agencies on the Preferred Supplier list may simply not be able to get their hands on enough qualified staff. Rates rise rapidly across the industry as contractors get the upper hand. Sometimes companies do not realize what has happened. The last time they took on a contractor they could take their pick. This time they have less choice and are being asked to pay more. It is the agency's job to explain to the client that the market has turned and the boot is now on the other foot. Until the next downturn, that is.

Who are the Contract Workers?

Articles in the press about contract work often start from the premise that everyone would rather have a permanent job than a series of contracts and that people are pushed into contract work through redundancy and ruthless employment practices.

This view may reflect more about journalists' own anxieties than the realities of contract work in many industries. Surveys of contractors in various industries repeatedly show that their motivation is overwhelmingly positive – money, independence, avoiding office politics, flexibility, variety and developing skills are all mentioned.

Let us try to get a picture of the kind of people who opt for long-term contract work rather than permanent employment. What motivates them and what qualities do they need to survive successfully as a contract worker?

Highly Skilled and Experienced   Almost by definition, contract workers are highly skilled. This is because employers in any industry use contractors to provide skills and expertise which they need but do not have in-house. This 'outsourcing', as it is called, is a growing phenomenon. It makes a lot of sense for organizations to employ expensive specialist staff only when they need them. Furthermore, by using contractors employers can take their pick of expert, highly skilled staff to take on someone whose skills and experience exactly match those needed on a specific project. This allows a closer fit between the project requirements and the personnel available than is possible if the company has to choose from its pool of permanent staff.

In addition, there is a bias in most contract markets towards specific skills rather than general experience, such as 'people management'. Many contract workers at managerial level identify themselves as project managers. This is partly because a great deal of contract work is project-based, but also because 'manager' is a vague term whereas 'project manager' is not. You can assess and quantify a project manager's skills and experience. More to the point, an agency can store these skills in its database using a number of keywords, so that when a contract comes in, a skills matching process can be carried out and suitable candidates identified automatically.

By and large, agencies have far too many CVs to hand-match candidates and vacancies – the process is more like computer dating than a personalized introduction service. For this reason, people with well-defined skills tend to get more work than those with experience which is generalized and hard to define, no matter how valuable that experience is.

A process of self-selection is also at work in making the contract market a highly skilled one. People thinking of moving into contract-working know that they are expected to be productive from day one of the contract. There will be no training, induction or honeymoon period. If they can't hack it, they'll be out. So people moving into contract work tend to be those who are highly skilled and already have a track record in the industry. And that leads us directly to the next quality you'll find in most contract workers: self-confidence.

Self-confident   Clearly, people who are worried about their ability to do their jobs, or those who feel they lack skills and experience, are not going to expose themselves to the rigours of the contract market. Contract workers have to have enough confidence to survive the knocks that are an inherent part of the contractor's life. Whereas permanent employees go for interviews only when they decide to change jobs, many contract workers go through the interview and selection process several times a year. There is no better way to assess how marketable you are. There is competition for most contracts – for plum assignments the competition can be fierce. You have to be able to survive the disappointments without losing confidence in yourself.

In most industries the contract market is not a market for novices. Because you are expected to be able to do the job immediately, there are no opportunities to pick it up as you go along. So contract work is not suitable for recent graduates who lack experience. They need to get experience with an employer, so that their CV reflects actual projects and skills, before they think of contract-working.

Earlier, we looked at the way that the contract market in many industries is project-based. This means that successful contract workers tend to be those who can demonstrate success in project work: in other words they are goal-oriented, able to work in a team, able to withstand the pressure of deadlines and so on. Clearly, they must also be able to cope with change, since the location they work in, their colleagues, the work they are doing and their pay levels are subject to frequent change. This is also true for professionals such as teachers; once they have signed on at an agency, they have to be constantly ready to get to grips with the next new school.

It works the other way too. Contractors are only as good as their last project; their work is under constant review by their employer or agency and if they do not measure up they do not get put forward for another contract.

Averse to Office Politics

Contractors like change. They are not 'organization' people. In one survey of contract workers, dislike of office politics was the third most frequent reason given for choosing contract work.

Many contractors loathe office politics and are only too glad to escape the endless round of meetings, manoeuvring, empire building and backstabbing that form the working week for many permanent employees. It is remarkable, as a contractor, how few meetings you have to attend. Those you do go to tend to keep to the point and be reasonably brief. The chief reason for this is that in teams brought together for the duration of a project, often consisting mostly of contractors from a selection of different agencies or companies, there is insufficient time for entrenched positions to develop or for simmering feuds to be politely acted out.

Take this personality element out of meetings and it is remarkable how short and productive they can be. Since the contractors have a fixed rate contract, none of them is looking for promotion, jockeying for position or trying to score brownie points. Conversation tends to restrict itself to the practicalities of the work in hand, a blessed relief to anyone who has had to sit through the mixture of group therapy and farce which characterizes so many departmental meetings for permanent employees.

Not 'Organization' People

Contract workers don't know who is 'in' and who is 'out' in the organization and couldn't care less anyway; they don't realize that Fred and Mary are not on speaking terms; they were not at the last Christmas party where Tom made a fool of himself; and they are often uninterested in what their job title is, which department they have been assigned to or who their boss is, except for the purposes of writing the boss's name on the time-sheet in order to get paid.

If contractors are working in an office, they will frequently not be on the distribution lists for company memos and information. Their email group will probably be set to receive only mail relevant to the project. They exist outside the dramas of office and organizational life. And this is part of the reason that managers like using contractors: it offers managers a fresh start, with a group of people who don't have preconceptions about them, the organization or the project.

The corollary of this is that contractors do not get any of the social 'benefits' of working in an organization. It is not unusual to watch the whole floor empty on a Friday lunchtime as all the permanent staff go off for a drink to which you, either from forgetfulness or exclusivity, have not been invited. Full-time employees may see Janet the contractor as not worth investing any social effort in, because she is only going to be around for three months, probably doesn't live locally and anyway is an 'outsider'.

This brings us to the topic of relationships between contractors and full-time employees. Full-time employees can find themselves working next to contractors who may be earning much more than they are for doing a similar job. This is bound to cause some resentment. Furthermore, 'presenteeism' (the practice of arriving early and staying late to persuade your boss not to sack you) has been growing during the recession.

Yet, as a contractor, you are paid by the hour, the day or the week. You work exactly the hours stated in your contract. If overtime is required, it is paid. None of the inducements – promotion, a better car, keeping your job – which persuade 'permies' to put in extra unpaid hours, apply to the contractor. So not only is the contractor being paid more than the permanent rate – he or she typically arrives two minutes before their charted time, takes exactly one unpaid hour for lunch, then leaves one minute after completing the contracted hours. The security of the permanent employee's job is supposed to make up for the long hours and lower pay. But many six-month contracts have an in-built notice period – the same period as that 'enjoyed' by many permanent workers.

Inexorably, those permanent workers who are skilled, mobile and undaunted by insecurity take note and fax their CVs off to the agency employing the contractors. And it is not unknown for them to leave the organization they are in, take to contract-working and end up some months later back in the same organization on double the pay with a shorter working week. After all, once they are contract-working, their experience in the company simply adds to their suitability for contract work within it.

In some areas of industry where skills are in demand, this is leading to a situation where permanent jobs are becoming the preserve of those who have no choice but to take them – the newly qualified; those who are not mobile; those who need to update or change their skills within an organization that will pay for training; and those who are frightened by the insecurity of project work. In this situation, pay levels for permanent jobs decline further, because these people do not have much bargaining power. Contract work rates look even more attractive by comparison, and the whole cycle reinforces itself.

Mobile　We have just seen that your mobility can affect your chances of working successfully as a contractor. Because most contract workers work for a variety of employers, they have to be able to travel. If you are not going to be completely miserable as a contract worker, you need to set your own limits on how far and how often you are prepared to travel in order to get work. This will largely depend on your personal circumstances, but working away from home is one of the big drawbacks contractors often mention when they are discussing their work.

Opportunistic　For most contractors, 'promotion' is not a meaningful concept. Each project or piece of work is evaluated as it comes along as a good or bad prospect. Once it becomes a reality, it is either a 'pot of jam' or a 'turkey'. 'Pots of jam' are well-paid, don't involve too much travelling, are not based in some dreary identikit town, and, most importantly, give you extra skills. (While contractors are expected to be proficient from day one, they love contracts which give them a chance to add something extra to their CV – supplementary skills, or a chance to apply existing skills in a different context or using new equipment.) A 'turkey' gives you no chance to learn anything, is based in a nasty building on a business park miles from anywhere and is poorly paid.

Now some contractors, stuck with a six-month contract from Agency A which has turned out to be a 'turkey', check the notice period on the contract, then quietly make themselves available again to agencies other than Agency A. Let us say that with the usual 'trip to the dentist' excuse they attend an interview for a better paid, more congenial contract available from Agency B. Agency B later phones to say they have an offer. The contractor gives notice to the turkey farm and heads for the jam factory. Is this unethical? Agency A will probably squeal with protest (of course it *never* poaches contract staff from other projects). Will they vow never to deal with this person again? No – because the contract market is skills-driven. And if Agency A finds itself with a contract that only this contractor can fulfil, it will tend to develop a forgiving attitude to any previous misdemeanours.

Ethical (More or Less)

On the subject of skills, the nature of some contract markets poses some problems for the ethical contractor and major opportunities for the totally unethical. Some agencies, such as those supplying medical and educational staff, check out qualifications and references extremely carefully. But many agencies in other industries do not.

A couple of years ago, with a lot of effort in terms of time and stress, I completed a part-time MSc and added it to my CV. This has turned out to be an excellent move in terms of career enhancement. Whenever I go for a contract the interviewers ask me about what I did on the course, and it has definitely made me more marketable. However, I have never been asked by an agency or an employer to produce the certificate or any other proof that I actually completed the course. And it has crossed my mind that someone *really* unethical would have to do no more than phone up the university for a course outline, mug up a few key terms – *et voila!* A further degree on your CV without any of the expense or effort. How many people are there in the contract market in various industries who do not have any of the qualifications they claim to have?

The same applies to project experience – if you say on your CV that you have done 16 projects, who is going to check them out to see whether you're telling the truth? Think of the practical problems involved in doing this. The project manager may well also have been a contractor, and has probably since moved to another contract, so there is no point trying to ask him or her. The project team has disbanded, and the contractor probably does not even know which department the project was in, let alone who the permanent manager was.

Imagine a recruitment agency trying to find its way round a major organization to check that a project really happened and that Joe Bloggs was on it – how many phone calls would this take? And that's just for one project. Contractors may list dozens of projects on their CVs. Checking that they really have the experience they say they have is virtually impossible. What's more, it is complicated by a further factor: contractors are usually unwilling to give one agency as a referee for another agency. Agency A asks for some proof that you really spent six months at Megacorp doing a brilliant job. But you got this job through Agency A's arch-rivals, Agency B. The whole thing is impossible. And that's without taking into account organizations like the collapsed bank BCCI. If you had no experience and felt like inventing a couple of years with them, who would be able to say differently?

As we said, some agencies, especially those supplying health and education staff, ask for references before they add you to their database, or before they actually give you a contract. The Employment Agencies Act specifically states that agencies must 'make enquiries to ensure that workers possess any qualifications required by law'. But many agencies do not check unless the law specifically requires them to. To a traditionalist this probably sounds appalling – a conman's charter. But how bad is it in practice?

In office-based contract work, you are not taking up a position in society, as you are when you get a permanent job. You are simply selling your expertise. If you can do the job, no one will be interested whether your qualifications are for real (brain surgery possibly excepted). As a contract worker you are only as good as your last project – all the genuine qualifications in the world won't get you work if you cannot actually do the job; exaggeration in the further degree department will go unquestioned if you can.

Not Part of Traditional Work Structures

There is a real sense in which contract workers exist outside the traditional structures of work and society, in which people's jobs define their place in the community, their social position and their identity. In the traditional model, you take a permanent job and become part of a work-based community. You socialize with your workmates: you go to their houses and they come to yours. You are therefore expected to live in a way that they can identify with – to have a house in a reasonably respectable area to ask them to; to put on dinner parties; to drive a newish car; to go on the kind of holiday they go on; to send your children to the kind of school they send theirs to.

All of this is in fact an enormous pressure to conform. A great deal of people's salary is taken up in maintaining a social position that is both dependent on, and a product of, their jobs. These are the kinds of people who are hit terribly hard by redundancy, because their work identity defines their social and personal identity – what they wear and eat, where they live and so on. When they lose their jobs, they lose everything. A contractor exists outside this network of social relationships. Working at an organization for three or six months, the contractor is highly paid yet is not expected to maintain a social position which demonstrates this fact. The contractor has no place in the organizational hierarchy, with its almost feudal relationships.

Because contract staff move around so much and tend not to find their friends through work, they are likely to have a fairly diverse circle of friends, met through leisure or local activities. In other words, because they don't socialize with a work peer group they have no one to show off to. So you find many contractors who, instead of buying a house on an executive estate, driving a new car and holidaying in the Caribbean, use their money in more idiosyncratic ways. I have met contractors who are taking flying lessons, buying pubs, taking six months off to play jazz, or using the intervals between contracts to write a novel.

So, for all the constraints and insecurities of contract work, it is enabling a lot of people to do what they want with their lives and freeing them from the pressure to have the same houses, cars, holidays and clothes as the people they work with. Instead, they can consider themselves much more as individuals and give real thought to what they want to do with their earnings. If they decide to drive their money, live in it or wear it, fair enough; but a surprising number of contractors choose less conventional ways of spending. They choose to *experience* their money in preference to being obedient consumers of more and better products.

After all, what's the point in having a great flat when you're working a contract 200 miles away and spending four nights a week in a hotel? And what contract worker wants to be mortgaged up to the hilt anyway? Most of them leave a huge safety margin and live in reasonably modest houses, especially since they cannot get as much finance as permanent employees can. (And this fact only goes to increase their disposable income.) What is the point in dressing to impress when you know perfectly well that the organization has bought your skills, not you as a person? What is the point in having a really smart car if you are slightly embarrassed to park it in the company car park and it is also a taxable perk?

Badly Served by Existing Institutions

In many ways, contract workers in skills shortage areas are a privileged group. They are highly paid and in demand. But they are also a group who are badly served by many of our institutions. The National Health Service, for instance, still assumes we all work for organizations like – well, the National Health Service – and can simply book a medical appointment or take half a day's paid leave – a topic we look at in Chapter 7.

Nor do the building societies serve contractors well. We shall also look at this topic in more detail in Chapter 7. Let us just mention here that some contractors that I have spoken to have the general attitude, 'OK, so the building society won't give me a mortgage, so stuff the building society. I'll save up and buy what I want for cash. And guess where I won't be putting my savings?'.

Private hospital plans are another area that lots of contractors have ambivalent feelings about. A lot of contractors carry permanent health insurance or critical illness cover, but far fewer belong to schemes such as BUPA. Partly, such schemes are identified with feather-bedded permanent employees on executive housing estates – exactly the kind of lifestyle that a lot of contractors have decided not to buy into. But there are more practical reasons – since contractors lose money when they're off sick, the last thing they want to join is a health scheme whose main benefit is that you get to spend lots of time in a hospital, even a nicely carpeted private one.

The Shape of Things to Come

The growth in contract work is set to continue, and with it the segmentation of the workforce into those with marketable skills and those with none. We may well see the growth of the 'virtual' organization, which has no permanent staff except for a small number whose job is to manage changing teams of contractors working on a variety of projects.

The market-driven nature of contract work will bring huge bonuses for those in skill shortage areas, but may well depress rates for those where supply of labour exceeds demand for it (such as many jobs in the media). It is also possible for the same person to be on both sides of this particular fence at different stages in their career.

John McDonald, a researcher who used to be a highly paid private industry contractor has now chosen poorly paid contract research work in a prestigious university department. Why? *'I feel comfier. And I loathe dealing with ghastly recruitment consultants.'* Well, recruitment consultants are a much maligned breed – we'll examine the work they do in Chapter 4. For now, it is worth remembering that many people are looking for interest and congeniality from their work, rather than maximum financial reward.

In the following chapters, we shall look at how to get contract work, how to deal with the payment side of things, and the kind of impact contract-working will have on your life. In Part 4 you will find an industry look-up section with details of agencies and contract working practices across a wide range of industries.

PART 2

Getting Down to Business

2 How to Find Contract Work

There are several different kinds of contract work, so we shall start this chapter by focusing on which kind we are talking about. Contract work *could* include:

1. A 'supply of services' contract via an agency.

2. A direct arrangement with the client in which you are self-employed and invoice the client.

3. PAYE contracting through an agency – you work on contract, but you are not self-employed, i.e. you are an employee of the agency.

4. PAYE contracts, i.e. short-term contracts in which the client pays you as an employee.

5. Non-agency third-party arrangements – you work freelance, for example for a production company which is in turn contracted to a TV company.

Options 3 and 4 are not really within the scope of this book, although we shall mention them in the context of other topics. They offer the worst of all possible worlds – all the insecurity and short-termism of 'real' contract-working, usually without the rewards in terms of increased pay. These kinds of arrangement are in any case less common in professional contracting, where skills are at a premium and agencies are competing to attract contractors.

Option 5 is an arrangement that tends to apply particularly in the media, where a TV company may issue a contract to a director or production company who in turn takes on freelances. There is more information on this in the media look-up in Part 4. We shall concentrate on the 'true' contract market-place, which is primarily covered by options 1 and 2.

Why Agencies Dominate the Market

The reason that agencies will dominate this chapter is that the growth in the number of agencies is an inevitable part of the growth in contract work. It is even true to say that the existence of agencies helps to expand the contract market. There are two reasons for this. Firstly, like any agency, recruitment agencies are primarily a selling operation. They get out into the market-place, doing the difficult (and often under-appreciated) business of persuading companies to use contractors. Secondly, they offer a viable way for large organizations to use contractors. Imagine an organization like BT trying to deal with contractors on an individual basis. It would be impossible, and would defeat one of the prime objectives in using such people, which is to reduce administrative overheads. It is far better for companies to select agencies and let the agencies handle recruitment, advertising, interviewing and all the rest of it.

In some sectors, the contract market has been established for a long time. When I worked in a government department in the late 1970s there were contract computer programmers (the fact that their agency was known in the department as 'Rent-a-Drunk' is neither here nor there). Now that there are hundreds of IT agencies, practices in the market have had time to develop, and there are two thick magazines devoted to nothing except the contract IT market.

For contrast, let us look at the contract or 'locum' social worker market, which is far less developed. There are only a handful of agencies, and they advertise in the back of magazines such as *Community Care*. There are only a couple of large operators, although they report that the market is growing. It is instructive to look at the growth in the contract IT market, because it has developed already and is a good place to look for clues as to how the contract market-place in other industry sectors might develop.

Scenario: How a Contract Market Develops

Undeveloped Contract Market

- At first, contractors are used in well-defined roles, mostly in the middle layers of an organization, when there is exceptional pressure of work or a need for specialist skills.

- There are one or two agencies which advertise in the professional press.

Developing Contract Market

- Gradually, the industry gets used to using contractors. The range of work undertaken by contractors expands. They begin to be used in roles such as project, line and senior management, which would not previously have been considered suitable. Some organizations implement a 'core staff supplemented by contractors' staffing policy.

- As the opportunities expand and more permanent employees work alongside contractors and see the opportunities, more employees move into contract work and the pool of available labour expands.

- At the same time, the more entrepreneurial contractors realize that they have both client contacts and a network of contractor colleagues. They set up agencies to capitalize on this expertise.

- The number of agencies starts to grow and their marketing to clients actually expands the contract market.

- A publisher of professional newspapers and magazines for an industry looks at the proliferating number of competing agencies and realizes that there is potential for selling advertising space regularly to agencies and other service providers, such as accountants. They establish a magazine aimed directly at contractors in a particular market.

Fully Developed Contract Market

- The number of agencies continues to grow and competition between them intensifies. Some are forced to cut their margins to stay in business.

- A competing publication sets up shop, aiming at exactly the same contractor/agency market.

- The contract market in this sector is now mature. Takeovers and amalgamations of agencies become common as larger agencies swallow smaller ones. The market begins to segment into established giant agencies on the one hand and start-ups on the other. Medium-sized agencies find themselves squeezed – undercut by small agencies and muscled out by large ones.

- Trade publishers start to add World-Wide Web sites to their operation so that contractors can use the Internet for on-line job searching. (So it is likely that some of the less developed contract markets will miss out or scale down the paper publishing steps and trade as on-line services from the outset.)

I have included this scenario for two reasons. Firstly, as contractors we must live in the future, not in the present. Always have your eye on what things are going to be like in 3–5 years' time. That way, you are not letting yourself in for any nasty surprises down the line. You can look at the scenario and work out where in this cycle your industry currently is. Secondly, it alerts those of you with an entrepreneurial streak (and most contractors have one) to some very good business opportunities – not in IT, which is well catered for, but in some of the developing contract markets which are ready for new agencies and specialist publications.

Notably absent from this scenario are the High Street agencies. With a few exceptions, they tend not to figure in the professional contract market. This has a lot to do with the specialized nature of the market. The people in the agencies are supplying specialist contractors for professional roles, so they themselves have to have a professional knowledge of the sector. The High Street agencies are not really in this professional market. In fact, the whole idea of shopping for a contract in the High Street would seem archaic to a lot of contractors. They are phoning, faxing, emailing and visiting Web job sites to get work.

Is it a Free-for-All?

Despite what you might think, not really. Employment agencies no longer need to register with the Department of Employment, but they are still regulated by the Employment Agencies Act 1973. The Department of Employment issues a booklet which summarizes the regulations governing how agencies must operate. In addition, it publishes another booklet which every contractor hopes they won't have to order, called *Trouble with an Agency?* But we'll come to *that* later.

Both booklets are free from the addresses given later in this chapter and both are reasonably straightforward and easy to read. Here we shall just highlight a few points which specifically affect contractors.

The act that says that an agency:

> must give to a worker on entering their employment full details in writing of the terms and conditions of employment, including whether he or she is under contract of service or is self-employed, the kind of work he or she may be supplied to do and the minimum rates of pay for such work; subsequent changes agreed by the worker must also be given to him or her in writing.

The agency must also meet the following requirements:

- It must tell you what it knows about the hirer's (i.e. the client's) business, the kind of work that is available, the hours and the rate of pay.

- If there are qualifications required by law to do the work, the agency has to find out whether or not you have them.

- The agency must make sure that doing the work does not break the law.

- The agency must not prohibit or restrict its workers in any way from entering the direct employment of a hirer. (An interesting and surprising point this, since so many contracts have clauses forbidding contractors to work directly for clients. I suspect that these obey the letter of the law by adding a clause about compensating payment in the event of such an arrangement occurring.)

- Agencies cannot supply workers to replace employees who are engaged in an industrial dispute.

- Agencies cannot send a contractor to a client if the contractor was employed directly by the client within the previous six months, unless the contractor explicitly consents. Presumably this proviso is to stop employers sacking workers and taking them back on with lower pay and fewer rights via an agency. A more likely scenario these days in high-tech industries is the contractor returning to do the former permanent job, at double the pay. However, this proviso does protect those whose jobs are under threat.

And *crucially*:

- An agency cannot refuse to pay you because the client you were sent to has not paid the agency.

This is because the agency's contract with the client is entirely separate from its contract with you. Here's a real-life, but lightly disguised example:

An agency sends a contractor to do some publicity writing for a City firm bringing out a new product. Due to upheavals in the business, the new product is scrapped. The City firm tells both the agency and the contractor that it wants the agreement to cease immediately. The contractor and the agency each look up their respective contracts.

The contractor discovers that there is a four-week notice period. This is legally binding and the agency has no choice except to pay the contractor for the four weeks after the date on which they formally tell the contractor that they are terminating the contract.

The agency of course, covered itself by negotiating a four-week notice period on its contract with the City firm. The agency is well aware that it has a liability to pay the contractor whether or not it can get the money out of the client. So the agency starts making legalistic noises, probably without informing the contractor, who is blissfully ignorant of the rows going on in the background.

Finally, the City firm realizes that there is no way to get out of paying and decides to make the best of a bad job by keeping the contractor for another four weeks to tidy up the loose ends.

As I mentioned, all the huffing and puffing takes place between the agency and the firm's Human Resources Department. Neither the contractor nor the permanent team that the contractor works with knows what is going on. This is another great advantage of contract work – the business arrangements are handled by the agency, not by the contractor, so working relationships are not disrupted by administrative or financial problems.

There is also an interesting aspect of working abroad which is covered by the Act. This is that employment agencies should not send a worker abroad unless they have made arrangements to pay the worker's return fare when the job ends.

Because employment agencies are no longer registered, to some extent the controls on them have slackened. However, agencies can be prosecuted for infringing the Act, with fines of up to £5000. Furthermore, they can be banned from the employment agency business for up to 10 years.

If Things go Wrong…

The Act is enforced by the Employment Agency Standards Offices, which are regionally based. If you feel that you have been unfairly treated you can ring your nearest Employment Agency Standards Office and make a complaint. It will investigate and send you the result of the investigation in writing. If this is going to take longer than four weeks, you will get a written progress report. You can contact the Employment Agency Standards Offices at these addresses:

North and Scotland	City House Leeds LS1 4JH Tel: 0113 283 6539 Fax: 0113 283 6547
Midlands, South West and Wales	Cumberland House 200 Broad Street Birmingham B15 1PQ Tel: 0121 608 9744 Fax: 0121 608 9749
London and South East	Exchange House 60 Exchange Road Watford WD1 7HH Tel: 01923 210706 Fax: 01903 210622

If you have trouble with an agency your best bet is to talk to the agency first. Agency cultures differ – some are very pro-client and anti-contractor, others are the reverse, and yet others take the view that there are always two sides to every story and it is their job to conciliate between contractor and client. To what extent you decide to fight what you consider an injustice is largely a matter of your own temperament and your belief in yourself.

I have had only one bad experience, and on that occasion I simply decided not to get involved and vowed never to work for the agency again. As a contractor, you know how many contracts you have done which have delighted the client and agency. You just have to accept that some clients and agencies have a combination of culture and working practices that actually make it difficult to work well, while with others you feel you can really do a good job.

After you have done a few contracts you begin to see how organizations in the same sector can be vastly different to work for. (And this makes you realize what a limited outlook a lot of permanent employees have.) It's particularly noticeable that some companies have a strong blaming culture. When something goes wrong they are more interested in attaching blame, finding the culprits and punishing them than they are in putting things right. In other companies, when problems arise the energy is directed into troubleshooting and problem-solving – a 'let's get this problem out of the way and get on with it' approach.

In 'blaming culture' companies, employees are noticeably edgy, paranoid, prone to blame others for their mistakes and liable to push tricky pieces of work towards the contractor so that they do not have to take responsibility for any problems which arise.

Why Things Go Wrong   Typically, problems happen for the following kinds of reason:

- *The job is not suitable for a contractor*
  For example, a job which requires knowledge of a company's entire product range and a subtle appreciation of the nuances and relationships between different kinds of products in the range is not a suitable job to give a contractor. Contractors are expected to be productive from day one, yet they simply cannot acquire a 'feel' for this kind of thing overnight. Again, a job that has to be completed according to a complex set of company procedures and in which those procedures are undocumented but are part of company culture is not a suitable job for a contractor.

- *No clear briefing or parameters*
  A friend of mine worked on a contract for a large company in which there was no clear statement at the outset of what she was meant to do. Sure enough, week by week the project definition would change and more elements would be added. Her earlier work was never correct, since things had moved on several stages since it was done. She has since spoken to a number of ex-permanent employees of this company and they emphasized that it was not an enjoyable place to be a permanent employee either. One of the problems in this particular instance was that a permanent, junior project manager found it difficult to appreciate what the contractor did not know about the organization's culture and structure. And that brings us to the next point.

- *Organization is rule-bound and bureaucratic*
  In bureaucratic, rule-bound organizations, contractors operate at an enormous disadvantage simply because they do not know the rules or their way round the bureaucracy. Most organizations have changed a lot in the last few years and are far more oriented towards achieving goals. They are more outward-looking, more informal and more concerned with helping you to do the best job you can.

But there are still 'dinosaurs' out there, even in the high-tech industries. This is where the contractors' grapevine can be very helpful – an organization's reputation sometimes goes before it.

- *The organization's work is not structured in a suitable way*
  Contractors tend to be involved with specific projects. If an organization is not geared to project and team-based work it is unlikely to be making best use of any professional contractors it brings in.

- *The contractor does not do the job very well*
  Be honest; it happens – even to the best of us.

Federation of Recruitment and Employment Services (FRES)

FRES is the recruitment industry's own professional body. You frequently see the FRES logo on agency advertisements in contractors' publications. It is meant to reassure you that you are dealing with a proper professional agency, not a fly-by-night bucket shop operation. FRES has different divisions for the different industry sectors and the FRES meetings are often reported in the contractors' press. Agencies do get thrown out of FRES if they are considered to have breached FRES guidelines, so it is not simply a talking shop – it has teeth and can on occasion use them. So while the FRES logo does not tell you much more than that the agency has not *yet* been thrown out of FRES, at least it tells you that.

Using the Internet and the Web to Get Work

Needless to say, the IT industry has gone furthest and fastest down this path, but be aware that other industry and commercial sectors are following close behind. This is not the place for an explanation of what the Internet and the Web are. The daily and Sunday papers have been full of explanations of the Web, along with articles by some journalists ridiculing the idea that anything important is going on. We can leave the journalists to find out at leisure just how wrong they are. The important thing is that if you do not know about the Web and the Internet you had better go and find out, because they are going to have a big effect on the way contractors find work.

What is happening is that agencies are setting up on-line job shops which list all the available contracts they have. They are also subscribing to similar services run by the trade publications in their industry. At the most basic level, contractors can access on-line contract shops via email (electronic mail). Once they have accessed the contract shop and indicated that they want to receive information, new contract vacancies are emailed to them each morning. The contractor can either view these in the evening, using his or her own PC, or give a work email address and pick the mail up at work. After all, most contractors expect agencies to be able to phone them, even if they are working at a client site.

An alternative way of accessing on-line job information is to use a 'browser' to look at bulletin boards or pages placed on the Web by agencies. This method means that you can search on-line for contracts in areas that particularly interest you. There is more on this in the next chapter.

You can see the advantages from the agency's point of view: instead of having dozens of people handling phone calls from contractors, they can up- and download the information once or twice a day and everyone is almost immediately informed. Writing in the May 1995 issue of *Computer Contractor*, John Samson predicted: 'This method of advertising is so rapid and cost-effective that the take-up by agencies is likely to approach 100%'. And this is a particularly powerful medium when linked with a CV emailed by return by the contractor.

The history of developing communications – the carrier pigeon, postal service, telephone, fax and now email – tends to show that the fastest method of communicating rapidly becomes the standard method of communicating. In the world of employment, responding quickly can often secure work. Contractors who can download vacancies, see one they like the look of and respond with an updated CV minutes later are clearly at an advantage.

Early on, there was a problem with using the Internet, as this comment from a computer contractor makes clear:

> Initially, some of the agencies using the Internet were disappointed with the response – because lots of students used the Internet in the early days, they got a lot of student CVs which weren't really suitable for contract vacancies. But that's changed as Internet access has broadened out.

One key advantage of a personal email address is that it does not change when you change contracts, move house or have to travel during the week – so you can stay in touch with the minimum disruption. And if you are after a contract anywhere in a different time zone, such as the USA or Australia, email is the ideal way to communicate at times that are convenient for both parties.

The next big development may be videoconferencing, which is also beginning to be used as a way for clients to interview contractors wherever they are.

Preferred Supplier Agreements

As you explore the contract market for your particular profession, you may come across the Preferred Supplier Agreement. This is an arrangement in which an organization invites a number of agencies to compete in order to become Preferred Suppliers – that is they will be called first when a contract vacancy occurs, and no competitors will be called unless the agency is unable to supply a suitable contractor. The company picks between one and half a dozen agencies for its Preferred Supplier list – sometimes it may need a number of agencies because of specialist requirements. So is this undiluted good news for the agencies on the list, or is there a catch?

The catch is that a PSA can be accompanied by a squeeze on rates. The company basically says, 'Yes, we'll give you the business, but in return for what you save on marketing, we want lower rates'. Yet agencies are competing in an open market-place for contractors, so they cannot just pass on lower rates or they will not attract enough contractors. After all, the contractor is not going to accept a lower rate just because the agency has negotiated a PSA – this is of no interest at all to the contractor.

The result? The agency has no option but to squeeze its profit margin. Where Preferred Supplier lists are built purely on the basis of price, the agencies sometimes *have* to lower rates to contractors, with the result that they get those contractors who have no choice but to accept a lower rate. However, some specialist departments in organizations have rebelled against the accountants, and are now insisting that the PSA should reflect the quality of the contractors offered, not simply their cost.

Some agencies have adopted the PSA practice and put favoured contractors on a Preferred Supplier list. But there is less benefit in this arrangement to contractors, and most of these agency/contractor PSAs operate more or less in name only. In a recent survey in *Computer Contractor*, only 1% of contractors thought that a PSA was an important factor in choosing an agency.

Good and Bad Agencies

Because more or less anyone can sell recruitment services, there are inevitably some goats among the agency sheep. Bad agencies do not tend to survive very long, because word travels fast among contractors, who begin to avoid them. This means that the agency has less choice about who to send out on projects, with the inevitable result that the clients also become dissatisfied. Reputation is a major business asset for an agency, and most want to be well regarded by both contractors and clients.

So what can you, the contractor, reasonably expect an agency to do for you? And how can you tell a good agency from a bad one?

1. A good agency is professional in its dealings
Your initial point of contact with an agency will almost certainly be a telephone call. If you are alert you can tell a lot about the agency from this call.

- Is the phone answered promptly and efficiently?

- Are you put through to a consultant dealing in your area, or are you passed around the office? If the agency does not know who you should be talking to, it is unlikely to have a very focused approach to getting you work.

- Does the recruitment consultant sound professional? After all, these people *are* the agency, and they probably deal with clients as well as contractors. You can reasonably expect them to be both courteous and friendly. Naturally, if they're any good at what they do, they are also busy, so do not expect to have a general chat about the state of the world with them.

- Does the agency ask for references?
- Does the agency confirm its contact with you?

2. A good agency understands the work you do
The recruitment consultant should be able to demonstrate a good knowledge of the work roles, specialist expertise, structures and technology which apply to your work area. Otherwise, how are they going to persuade clients to give them decent contracts, or place you in a position which matches your skills?

3. A good agency is straightforward
The recruitment consultant should be prepared to discuss rates. Obviously, rates vary from one project to another, even for people with the same skills, so the consultant will not make any commitment on rates. But the consultant should be willing to indicate the range of rates that currently applies. In fact, this is often a good test of whether the consultant is a 'doer', keen to make a deal, or simply a talker. By the same token, you should be willing to put a price on your own matchless talents and state the amount you're hoping to get. You too can discuss a range of rates. One good way of approaching this is to say, 'Well, over the last year I've worked on several projects and the rates have varied from £x to £y per hour. Does that range sound about typical?'.

What is *not* acceptable to a professional contractor is the blanket refusal to discuss rates, which is practised by a small minority of less professional agencies. These agencies insist that you set your own rate, clearly hoping you will underbid the market and that they will be able to pocket a huge differential. The more professional agencies set margins which are frequently revealed to the client. These agencies will tell you if you are quoting rates way below or above the market. In fact, some agencies present a list of contractors to the client, showing the rates each contractor will be charged at. These agencies are as keen as you are to get better rates, because that increases their percentage commission. Most professional contractors feel more comfortable with this way of working, and it is far less exploitative than being forced to quote a rate to an agency, which may bear no relation to the rate the agency is charging the client.

4. A good agency is a good payer
If an agency says it will post you a cheque it *may* be because it is a small operation with not many contractors on its books. Most agencies ask you for your bank details and then pay by BACS (Bank Automated Clearing System) straight into your account. (In fact, they are responsible for coining the new verb 'to bacs', meaning to pay you electronically, as in 'invoice us and we'll bacs you 10 days later'.)

Good agencies pay promptly. They see this as part of the package they can offer to attract good contractors. Remember that the period from when you do the work until the money goes into your account is a time of risk for you. If the agency goes bust you will not see your money. Try to control this situation by invoicing as often as they will let you – weekly if possible – so that the amounts you are waiting for are smaller.

5. A good agency usually has a high profile
This is not always true – some very high-powered agencies are very discreet – but they are the exception. Most agencies that are worth bothering with advertise frequently in the professional press. Larger agencies will advertise in every issue (one of the ways in which they grow faster).

6. A good agency is in it for the long term

Of course, all agencies have to start at some time. But try to develop a sense for those agencies that are committed to a long-term presence in the market and those that are the brainchild of a few disaffected recruitment consultants taking a flyer on a skills shortage. It is worth reading the 'Agency News' section in your professional press, if there is one. While this often simply reprints public relations puffs from agencies, it also tells you which agencies are expanding and gives hints about which agencies have lost important clients (and may therefore be contracting in a more literal sense).

7. A good agency has some commitment to quality of service

It is difficult to tell in advance whether an agency is committed to providing a good quality service, and once you have found out that it isn't it is a bit late to do anything with the knowledge except tell your friends. Some agencies go in for quality schemes, such as BS 5750 or Investors in People. There is a good deal of cynicism about these schemes among both agencies and contractors, but if an agency has bothered to go in for one of them it does at least indicate that it is *aware* of the issue.

How to Find Agencies

There are a number of ways of finding out the names of agencies which operate in your area.

Telephone the Specialist Publishers

EMAP and VNU are two big names in the world of specialist professional publishing. Call them and ask firstly whether there is a professional publication for your work area, and secondly whether there is any magazine specifically aimed at contractors in your work area.

EMAP: Tel. 0181 441 6644
VNU: Tel. 0171 316 9000

Visit a Large Newsagent

Visit a large branch of W. H. Smith or a similar newsagent. The bigger branches of Smiths carry a range of trade and professional publications grouped in their own section. Browsing through the back pages of these can set you in the right direction for finding an agency relevant to you.

Surf the Net, Wander the Web

Find out about on-line jobs. Additionally, you can leave messages on relevant bulletin boards and sites to make contact with other contractors in your professional area who can help you get started.

Use People Networks

If you are working with contractors, ask them which agencies they use and which they consider to be the best. Ask friends to ask their friends – follow up any contacts you make.

Telephone Organizations Directly

Call an organization you might be interested in working for as a contractor. Talk to someone in the Human Resources department and ask if the organization ever uses contractors and if so which agencies they tend to come from.

Carry Out a
Newspaper
Survey

Lots of agencies advertise in the national press. Decide which newspapers would be likely to carry agency advertisements relevant to you. Phone their Advertising Departments and find out on which day they carry the advertisements and editorial that are relevant to your professional area. For two weeks, buy every edition that is relevant and file the agency advertisements.

Once you have located the sources of contract work, the next stage is to go about actually getting a contract. As sure as eggs are eggs, your thoughts are turning to your CV. In the next chapter we shall take a look at the myths and realities of CV preparation in the contract market.

3 How to Get a Contract

The Great CV Myth

Traditional job advice – and there is plenty of it around – often boils down to a lengthy lecture on how to write your CV. In this chapter, we shall look at why that advice no longer applies and why the CV is both more, and less, important than it was.

The kind of advice on job hunting that you will find in your High Street book store runs along these lines. Think carefully about the employer's requirements. Compile a job history which highlights your skills and aptitudes. Word process it nicely. Then send it off hopefully and wait. Right?

Wrong. This game is OK if you are applying for a permanent job, but for a contract professional after a well-paid contract, it is a dead loss.

For one thing, it is too passive. To get a contract, you need to engage with the people who have the work. It is not like the process of applying for an advertised job, where the Personnel Department is going to check each CV against the requirements of a specific post. You send your CV to Personnel, and the next communication is either a rejection or an interview. You may never speak to anyone in the organization.

Contract work is different. You need to market yourself much more actively and broadly. For contract workers who go through agencies there are no 'posts'. Instead, there are a number of agencies supplying people to work on specific projects.

So firstly you need to gather as much information as possible about those agencies:

- What kind of work do they have?
- Which is the biggest?
- What are their rates?
- How do they pay?
- How quickly do they pay?
- How often do they pay?
- Which are the new, hungry ones?
- What is the character of each agency?
- What is each one like to deal with?

You will not find this information in the local library; you will have to spend afternoons phoning round agencies and contract workers, gathering information about what is out there and how you fit in. So don't pick up your pen before you pick up the phone. And remember – you can turn these aspects of the new work to your advantage. When a specific job is advertised, you cannot really ring up and ask the employer what is wanted on the CV. But with an agency you can. The contract worker's CV is not based on guesswork; it is based on market research and self-knowledge.

That is the problem with traditional advice about the 'perfect' CV. It is too dependent on second guessing the person reading the CV. Why bother trying to guess what the person is looking for when you can just pick up the phone and ask? Then you can include those things on your CV, *knowing* that that is what they want.

What Happens to Your CV?

As a contract professional, your CV represents a data input form for an agency. Many agencies simply strip out the skills they're interested in, bin the paper copy and update their database. When they get what they call 'a requirement', i.e. a request from an employer, they run the requirement against their database of contractors, skills, locations and so on. A set of names is churned out, and if you are on the list, the agency then calls you to check (a) that you're available and (b) that it is OK to send your details to the company in question.

The agency then takes your details and those of the competing contractors, formats a CV in its own house style for each person and sends the CVs to the client. The CV you send to the agency is *not* a make or break document in these circumstances. It will never be seen by the client/employer. Your CV can be quite poorly presented, but the agency may like the look of your skills and add you to its database. When the agency sends out the CVs to the client they will all be in the same in-house format. The people who paid to have fancy CVs done will be no better off in terms of securing the contract than those who did it themselves.

So let the agency worry about the perfect CV for an employer. What the new worker should worry about is presenting a CV to the agency in such a way that it forms the basis of a great database entry. In the next section, we shall see why you should think more in terms of presenting yourself to a dating agency than constructing a record of your life.

The keys to a successful database entry are:

- Research

- Self-knowledge

- Feedback

- Skills, not self-advertisement

Sell Your Skills, Not Yourself

With traditional job applications you are selling yourself as much as your skills. 'Look', you say, 'not only do I have plenty of experience relevant to this specific job; I am also responsible, cheerful, a good team player and able to work on my own initiative.' We all know the formula.

But contract work changes the formula. If you are sick you will not be paid. If your work is not good your contract will be terminated. If your work is OK but you are a pain in the neck they will probably put up with you in the knowledge that you are only going to be around for three or six months and then they need never see you again.

So businesses which are offering contracts are not really buying into you *as a person*. They want to borrow your skills for a short period, usually for work on a specific project. During this period you may work on a team composed entirely of contractors. So it is very important that your CV is skills- and knowledge-oriented, rather than a commentary on the positions you have held and your general suitability.

In other words, forget the hobbies and the Rotary Club and the general staff development stuff. Play up skills, training and knowledge. Middle managers are precisely the people who have been squeezed out as organizations de-layer, so don't go on about *being* a manager. Make very specific points about having budget, project or people management *skills*. Preferably, show that you combine these with other skills. Most contract work is tied to specific projects and budgets, so if you are applying for management-type work your CV must demonstrate that you can handle projects, milestones, deliverables, budgets, deadlines and so on.

Tell Them   Because of the nature of contract work there is also
What They   some extra information which you *must* include. This
Want to Know   is to do with your availability. Most agencies dealing with contracts have national coverage. Much of their work is done over the telephone and they don't restrict their operations to the locality in which they are based. They usually hold details for contractors from all parts of the UK. Some also have European and US contracts, since many of the companies they supply are multinationals.

Therefore you must make clear where you are prepared to work. You can do this in several ways:

> Based Milton Keynes but can commute up to 1 hour each way.

or

> Based Milton Keynes but am prepared to stay away for short periods (contracts up to three months). Will therefore consider all locations, including Europe.

or

> Available for work in UK Midlands, South, South West.

or even

> Available for work in Milton Keynes.

(but don't expect the phone to ring very often).

A word of warning though. If you are a first-time contractor, be very cautious about arranging a lengthy contract which requires you to stay away from home. It sounds fine in theory to stay in a hotel during the week. But it can be insidiously alienating and depressing. Here's Alec, whose family lives in Suffolk but who had to work in Brighton for a year:

> The first night, you think, this is going to be fine. But by the third or fourth night you're staring at the wall of your bedroom wondering what's gone wrong with your life. It just gets to you – it's hard to explain why.

Many contractors have had exactly this experience and it does 'just get to you'. This is a major problem with contract-working. In many cases the work is not local and you are expected to be incredibly mobile to get it. Many contractors find life on their own in a small hotel so depressing that they commute miles by car to avoid it.

On-site and Off-site Work

There is also the question of on-site and off-site work. Most contract work is on-site – at the employer's premises or site. However, there is a small and slowly growing market for off-site work, which usually involves a combination of visits to the client and work at home. If you are interested in off-site work, say so on your CV. It is essential in this case to list the equipment relevant to your trade or profession which can help you work off-site. For a contract writer this might be:

> I am available for off-site work and can provide the following facilities: PC and word-processing software; printer; fax; modem; Internet connection.

Availability   Any agency will want to know when you are available. Many contractors give dates a week or two *before* they're really available, because they know that start dates can be delayed by sickness, holidays, administrative problems and so on.

Handling the   Let's imagine that you are an engineer with specialist
Call to the   knowledge of a design approach called ZOG3, mak-
Agency   ing your first approach to an agency:

Hi there. I'm an engineer and I wondered if I could talk to one of your consultants about my skills and whether they fit with the kinds of contracts you get.

(The receptionist transfers you to a consultant.)

Hello, John Smith speaking. What can I do for you?

Well I'm just ringing for some information really. I'm a ZOG3 engineer and I wondered if you have contracts for ZOG3 work.
We do usually have a few contracts for ZOG people. It's not as popular as NOG4 of course, but we do get them.

(No matter what skill you have, the consultant always implies that there is some much better skill that you should have. Take no notice: this is all part of the charm of the recruitment industry.)

Right. And do they tend to be all over the place or...
All over the place. Lots of ZOG3 sites in the City and we seem to have quite a few contracts in the Midlands at the moment. Where are you based?

Milton Keynes.
OK, so you're central. Prepared to travel?

Within reason, yes.
What, say an hour's commutable?

Yes.
Well, you should be able to get something. Got a live one in at the moment actually: Birmingham, ZOG3 with some project management.

Can I just ask you about rates?
You can ask.

I know rates vary from contractor to contractor, but can you give me a rough idea of the range that you might pay for ZOG3?
Well the lowest is probably round the thousand mark. Highest [deep intake of breath] – twelve hundred. But that's pushing it.

OK. That's been very helpful.
Fax us a copy of your CV. Or you can email it.

I will – shall I address it to you?
I'm on holiday for the next two weeks. Tell you what, send it to Mark Francis – he'll be covering the ZOG contracts while I'm away.

OK, thanks.

Building on the phone call

Now you can start writing your CV.

When you finally print it out you can customize a copy for this agency to highlight your ZOG3 Project Management expertise, your willingness to work in the City or the Midlands and any other relevant expertise in the City. You also have a named individual to send it to.

Log these details under the agency's name and move on to the next one. Gradually you will build up your own database of where the work is, how much it pays, what ancillary skills are important and so on. You will work out what the market is, how you fit into it and what your market worth is.

Getting Feedback on Your CV

Your work is not finished when you send off the CV. It is essential to follow it up and get feedback on it. Call the agency or employer and ask to speak to the person handling your area of work. Ask them these kinds of question:

- Did they get your CV?
- Do your skills seem relevant?
- Are you the right age?
- Is there any other information they need?

A professional recruitment agency will be very helpful about this – don't forget that the agents are on commission. They want to place you if your skills are relevant. If they don't feel they can do much for you, they would far rather tell you than have you ringing up every day asking whether there are any contracts.

When you phone for feedback, agencies will often print your database record and send it to you for checking. It looks nothing like a CV. One recruitment consultant described it as 'indexed on all the buzz-words we're interested in'. There are nearly always amendments and corrections you can make at this stage.

For example, one agency continually offered me contracts running computer Help Desks, something I have no experience of. When they sent me my database entry, I found that one of the lines on my CV – 'writing on-line help for software packages' – had been indexed as 'Help Desk'. So I was able to call them and get the entry fixed. Result? A call offering a contract writing on-line help for a software package.

ACTION LIST
Getting
Contract Work

- Be active

- Research the market

- Don't second guess requirements

- Target your CV at likely agencies

- Don't be too specific

- Sell your skills not yourself

- Be flexible

- Don't spend hours on the perfect CV

Lies, Damned Lies and CVs

So far, we have looked at the CV in terms of presenting your skills positively. But at what stage does positive presentation become overstatement, or even dishonesty? The contract recruitment industry is notoriously lax about checking out its contractors. The industry works on a 'suck it and see' principle. If a contractor is hopeless, he or she is not used again. This raises all kinds of questions about what you do and don't include on your CV. We touched on this briefly in Chapter 1. In the next section we shall take a look at the ethics of how you present yourself.

How closely your CV will be scrutinized depends on the sector you work in. Clearly, if you are applying for locum social work through a reputable agency like Social Workline, you are going to be carefully checked out. On the other hand, if you are a programmer in London and an IT agency in the Midlands has your CV, it may well take your CV on trust and may send you out for an interview with the client without ever meeting you personally.

Some of the agencies I spoke to while preparing this book had obviously had bad experiences, finding out the hard way that the contractor's CV was a work of fiction. On the other hand, most contractors could quite legitimately write their CVs up in a dozen different ways and each version would make them look like a person with a different set of skills. That is because people who have been working on projects for some time have a range of skills and experience (the portfolio career, described by writers like Charles Handy and others).

There is nothing dishonest about someone who has done both financial management and management training having three CVs: one which makes the person look like an ace financial manager; one in which the individual appears to be a dedicated training person; and a third which gives both equal weight.

A CV is not an identity card – try not to think of it as a definitive statement of who you are. Try in fact, not to think of 'my CV'. It should not be something you have laboured over and finalized and which is now set in stone. With the advent of personal computers there is no reason for it to be. Think instead of 'my skills set'. Every CV you send out should be a customized, edited version of the information you have stored about your skills and experience, directly focused on the agency or contract you are after. Let us emphasize the key points: A CV is *not*:

- an identity card
- a personal history
- a passport
- standardized
- vague
- untruthful
- out of date.

A CV *is*:

- updated after every contract
- sales literature
- focused and customized.

On-line CVs – Using Email

We saw in the last chapter that lots of agencies are moving their services on-line because it makes sense for them to receive CVs as emailed files rather than paper copies. It is faster too:

> If someone is using one of the proven word-processing packages, such as WordPerfect or Word version 6, then we can go into the email, save the CV to our word-processing package and start to manipulate that CV immediately.
>
> There is no need to scan the details into our system, or to reformat. Even with a good scanner and optical character recognition software it could take up to two hours to re-jig a CV, whereas with email it can be as little as half an hour.
>
> Mark Smith of Sharp Decisions, quoted in *Computer Contractor*, 12 May 1995.

The email revolution can be a wonderful thing for a contractor who is currently working as a permanent employee but who is making the first tentative approaches to agencies. It is embarrassing to make these kinds of call in an open-plan office, and many people take a day's holiday in order to make the initial agency contacts from home.

With email the process is (a) private and (b) silent. No one sitting near you knows that you were so fed up after the departmental meeting that you sat down and emailed your CV to an agency. This is not to say that your incoming and outgoing mail cannot be read by the computer system administrator – it can, so remember that this is a calculated risk. But imagine how many thousands of messages are processed each day in most organizations – what, realistically, are the chances of the administrator reading one or two messages out of all these?

The other excellent thing about email is that exchanges do not have to take place in 'real time'. You can send your CV to a recruitment consultant; the consultant can read it at a convenient time; you can follow it up immediately with a message without seeming pushy; the consultant can read your message and respond when he or she wants.

Of course, this is also the beauty of having your own email account with a provider such as CompuServe. People can email your personal account during the day and you can download the mail from your mailbox when you go home in the evening. If you do not use these services already, when you start you'll realize why people call the stuff that comes through letterboxes 'snail mail'. As contractors we owe it to ourselves to keep up to date with what's going on – if you don't have a PC, Internet access and an email service, think very seriously about getting them.

The whole process of getting yourself on-line used to be a complicated one, only suitable for technical enthusiasts, but CompuServe now has a service to help you do this. Of all the on-line services, I would recommend CompuServe if you are not a communications expert. In my opinion, they are the simplest to set up, easiest to use and most professional. If you don't have a modem, they will supply a cheap one, and they are used to dealing with non-technical people on the phone. And the computer contractors, who you would expect to know about these things, are fans.

Your Own Home Page on the Web

Lots of contractors who have been using on-line and Internet job services to look for contracts are now beginning to take the idea a stage further. Why not advertise themselves on the Internet (or to be strictly accurate, the Web)? You can set up what is known as a home page – a page of information written by you which can also contain jumps and links to other places. Interested agencies or clients can access this to get more information about you.

In the next chapter, we shall look at how to set about getting the work once you have found where it is.

4 Getting an Offer

There is a solid body of opinion among contractors that old estate agents never die, they just become recruitment consultants. Certainly, the job of an agency recruitment consultant calls for a lot of the same skills – the persuasive patter, the 'friendly' manner and the ability to close a deal quickly. And recruitment consultants occupy the same marshy middle ground as estate agents: whose interests are they really looking after (apart from their own, that is)?

Well, that's the cynical view and there is undoubtedly some truth in it. But contract-working would be a sad business if you only dealt with people like that. Incredibly, despite the long hours spent persuading contractors that six months in Slough represents the most fabulous career enhancement, some recruitment consultants manage to remain real people. 'Oh come on Paul', you say, 'This is me you're talking to, remember?', and if you've known him through contracts thick and thin, Paul finally cracks up, drops the patter and agrees to put a few pounds on the rate to compensate for the Slough aspect of things.

So what are they really like, these recruitment consultants, the people you have to negotiate with every time you contact an agency? Good recruitment consultants have a few things in common:

- They know the industry that they are dealing with.

- They are in it for the long term – so they know that there is no point bamboozling you into doing a contract you don't want, because they'll only end up picking up the pieces.

- They are energetic (well they should be – after all, they are on commission, always a good motivator).

- They are competitive – because agencies are nearly always competing to place contractors.

- They are as professional as the contractors they are placing.

- They are persistent.

- They have a sense of humour.

- They don't brood over the contract or contractor they lost – they get on to the next one.

- They are opportunistic – they can spot a contract opportunity a mile away.

- They are inquisitive – recruitment consultants need to be in the know, and they are always interested in who you are working for and through.

- They are ethical (well, as ethical as the contractors, anyway).

Lots of contractors think that recruitment consultants have an easy life. After all, they just have to make a couple of calls, then sit back and take a percentage while you actually do the work. So it is not unusual for contractors who are fed up to have a go at recruitment consultancy, at which point they discover that it is not quite as easy as it looks. The contractor may have plenty of industry knowledge and industry contacts, but unless he or she is comfortable with selling and has a fair number of the characteristics listed above, failure is inevitable.

And don't forget that the recruitment consultant's hours can be punishing. Contractors leave work promptly as soon as their hours are done, yet when they finally get home or back to the hotel, they may find the recruitment consultant calling them. The consultant knows that it is difficult for contractors to talk about new contracts at work, and if there is a live opportunity they want to collar the contractor before a rival agency does. So they have to get hold of the contractor in the evening. It's not that easy a life.

How Recruitment Consultants Operate

In Chapter 3, we looked at how agencies dealt with your CV when they received it – skill stripping it and loading it onto a database. But there are some rules, which most reputable agencies abide by, when it comes to the next part of the process.

- *Agencies should get your permission before they send your CV to a client*
  You may not want to work for the prospective client, or may have some legitimate reason for not wanting that client to see your CV (for example, the agent may have failed to notice that this is your first contract and you are currently a permanent employee of the client in question, in which case it would be slightly embarrassing for them to get your CV as a potential contractor). Far more importantly, another agency acting for the same client may have already sent your CV to the client, for this or another contract. There is more about this in the section 'Dealing with multiple agencies' below.

- *Agencies will want an updated CV*
  Any agency worth its salt will ask for a CV which includes the contract you are currently working on.

Agencies are not dealing in history – what you were doing six months ago. Don't be surprised to be asked for a new CV every couple of months; it helps them to give you a better service.

- *Agencies should tell you the rate before they send out your CV*
And not only the rate, but all other relevant considerations. For more information on this, see 'Negotiating the rate'. Here, we shall just comment that sometimes an agency is desperate to present a good set of CVs, or even any CV, to the client, to stop the client calling another agency. And it can be tempted to, let's say, 'overstate' the benefits of the contract in order to get you to agree to having your CV sent to the client while the agency plays for time and tries to rustle up more CVs.

Negotiating the Rate

The agency should know your general rates and should quote a specific hourly, daily or weekly rate to you when you begin discussing a contract – well before your CV has gone out.

How Much are You Worth?

The first step in carrying out an effective rate negotiation with an agency is to know what you are worth. This is easier said than done. Contractors tend to be very secretive about their own rates – if they are earning more than their fellow contractors, they will be unpopular, but if they are earning less they will feel stupid. By the same token, because contractors are constantly testing and reassessing their market worth, they are avid collectors of information about current rates.

One rough guide is permanent salaries in the same industry. Some highly skilled contractors reckon that to make contracting worthwhile they need to earn roughly double the monthly gross salary of a permanent employee doing the same job, so that will give you a rough idea. The relationship between permanent and contract rates of pay varies from one industry to another, but it is fairly easy to get agencies to quote ranges or to get them to say how much more an average contractor would earn than an average employee. From this information you can work out a rough daily or weekly rate for yourself.

Some agencies will actually chance a rate. They may think the rate you have quoted is high, but say, 'We'll put it to the client and if we lose it on price, so be it'. Quite often this is not such a high risk as they are making out – they will also be putting forward some less experienced contractor who is cheaper, so either way the agency will get its commission. It has to be said, though, that most clients do not choose the cheapest contractor – within reason, they choose the one they think will do the job best.

How Many Hours a Week? When you come to negotiating the nitty-gritty of a real live contract, you must also bear in mind some things which seem trivial but can make the difference between whether the contract is profitable or not. Chief among these is the length of the working week and the status of lunch hours. Suppose an agency phones you up and tells you about a great contract at £25.00 an hour for a 40 hour week – a grand a week. Yippee!

You go for an interview, get the contract and agree a start date. You tell other agencies that you are no

longer available as you are starting a new contract.
The written contract arrives and it states £25.00 an
hour for a 35-hour week. You investigate and find
that the agency has made a 'mistake' and either over-
stated the hours or assumed that lunch hours were
paid when they are not. This leaves you out of pocket
by £500.00 in every four-week period.

If you are having to pay heavy travelling expenses or
hotel bills, this may mean the difference between a
profit and a loss on the contract. Of course, if you have
not yet signed the contract you are not committed to
doing it, but you are now in a very awkward position;
you will have to let the client down, re-negotiate the
rate or drop the agency and re-circulate your CV. In
my experience, most of these muddles are caused by
genuine misunderstandings, partly caused by the fact
that so much of the contract negotiation is done by
telephone. But they are irritating, and the best advice
is to try to avoid them by asking the right questions
at an early stage.

*Invoicing and
Payment*
There are probably as many different combinations
of invoicing and payment arrangements as there are
agencies. Don't assume that professionals are paid
monthly. In IT contract-working, for instance, many
highly paid professional contractors drive a very
hard bargain with their agencies – and that includes
the right to invoice them weekly. Other agencies have
an 'invoicing day' – often the last Friday in the month.
Time-sheets (signed by the client) and invoices have
to arrive by the beginning of the following week and
are then processed. (Remember to take copies of
signed time-sheets before you send them off, in case
they get lost in the post.)

Most agencies now pay by BACS (for more details see
Chapter 2). Quite why some of them manage to pay

the day after receiving the invoice, while others hold onto your money for 30 days, is something of a mystery. It is a key point to consider when you are deciding how good an agency is. Do you want to lend them your money for anything up to two months, which is the case if you invoice monthly and they pay a month later? Remember that your money is at risk all the time the agency has it – if the agency goes bust you are very likely to lose it all. Choosing an agency that pays efficiently minimizes this risk.

Contract Start Date and Duration

There is nothing more maddening to contractors than to make a verbal agreement to start a contract, only to find the start date receding for these kinds of reason:

- The project manager has appendicitis.
- The software is not ready.
- The purchase order has not arrived.
- The budget has not been approved by the finance committee.

and so on.

You sit around earning nothing and racking up bills, wondering whether you ought to make yourself available again or if it will really start next Tuesday as promised. (See the interview with Luke Barnes on p. 137 for a real-life example of this happening to a contractor.) Again, the best thing to do is to work out your position in advance.

If the agency phones you to tell you that there is a delay, be understanding but explain that your CV is currently with other agencies and that if the delay is longer than a week (or however long you decide) you will have to reconsider your position. This is perfectly reasonable – it will hardly come as a big surprise to the recruitment consultant, who is probably already on the phone three times a day to the client, warning that its preferred contractor will walk unless it gets its act together. You can then phone other agencies and tell them that although you thought you had a firm contract, there seems to be a delay in the project starting, so could they reactivate your CV, just in case the project falls through altogether. You have now been honest with all parties and protected your own interests.

Other points to watch for are precisely how long the contract is – check the end date, because agents and clients do sometimes make mistakes. Check too whether the contract is for you to work every week between the specified dates, or only when needed. You need to know your position if there are delays once the contract has started.

Most agency contracts contain notice periods. This is the notice that the agency must give you before early termination of the contract. For contracts of up to three months this is often a week. For contracts of six months and over it is generally up to four weeks (which compares very well with the contracts of a lot of so-called permanent employees).

ACTION LIST
Negotiating a Rate

- Know what you are worth.

- Find out the hourly, daily or weekly rate.

- Find out if this includes or excludes lunch hours.

- Double check the length of the working week, and if possible check again at the interview.

- How often can you invoice?

- How quickly will you be paid?

- What is the start date?

- What is the duration of the contract?

- Are there likely to be any gaps, 'down-time' or lay-offs?

- What is the notice period?

Dealing with Multiple Agencies

Most contractors are registered with more than one agency. In highly developed fields such as IT, the average contractor is registered with 30 agencies. Towards the end of a contract, he or she begins ringing round the agencies and sending an updated CV, looking for the next contract. This is a difficult period. You can tell almost immediately how much work there is around from how many agencies want to send out your CV. What inevitably happens is that two or more opportunities arise at the same time, but from different agencies. One is a total turkey: miles from home, with an indifferent rate, and at a company or organization you are not very keen on. The next is a pot of jam: easy to get to, good rate, free lunches, nice client. The third is so-so.

Inevitably, the turkey farm is the first one to offer an interview. You go along reluctantly, because you are waiting for an interview at the jam factory. On the same day, you get an offer from one agency – the turkey farm is keen to have you – and an interview arrangement from another agency – the jam factory wants to see you. What do you do? Go for the bird in the hand even though it's a turkey? Turn it down and risk not getting the jammy one? In these circumstances contractors have been known to go to ground and hide until they've had the interview for the job they really want. This is difficult, as the recruitment consultant makes increasingly desperate attempts to get in touch with you.

As usual, honesty is the best policy. Tell the first agency that you are being interviewed for a position nearer home which you would prefer for obvious reasons. Nine times out of ten at this stage the agency asks how much the other job pays. Blushingly, you admit that yes, it is a slightly better rate now that they come to mention it. This is where the competitiveness of the agent comes in. If they think you're worth it and they know that you tell the truth, they will get straight on to the client and tell them that 'their' contractor has a better offer. This can result in the original client offering more money, and is one of the main reasons why the contract market is such a sensitive barometer of supply and demand in the labour market.

What you cannot do, especially if you work in a sector where there is only a handful of agencies, is to say yes to the contract and then pull out. That said, contractors do it all the time, but agencies really hate it and are likely to put you to the bottom of their lists if you do it more than once. The agency regards the verbal agreement you make on the phone as a contract. The written contract is simply a confirmation. There is not much they can do about it, but remember that people move around from one agency to the next and you may be getting yourself a bad reputation.

However, juggling two different contract offers from two different agencies is amateur stuff compared with the position you get into when two different agencies offer you the same contract. This situation arises because clients call several agencies in order to get a spread of rates and contractors. However, the same contractors tend to be registered at all the main agencies, and if they have the right skills for the job, theirs are the names that will pop up on the databases at every agency.

That is why agencies try to do everything as quickly as possible – they want to get to the contractors before their rivals. If you are a contractor, the ethical thing to do is to explain that you have already been called about this contract by Agency A and they are sending your CV. However, some agencies talk in such guarded terms 'a large company in the South of England' that you may not at first realize that Agency B is on about a contract that Agency A has already contacted you about. Correct Agency B as soon as possible and explain that you didn't immediately recognize the details.

So far so ethical. But suppose Agency B then enquires how much you have been offered? You are quite within your rights not to tell them, but Agency B's recruitment consultant is the persistent type and goes on to tell you what rate Agency B is offering. And to your amazement, it's far more than Agency A. This situation occurs quite frequently, and it has a number of underlying causes:

- Agency B may be a very small agency with very low overheads and correspondingly low margins. It can offer more to contractors because its own costs are lower.

- Conversely, Agency B may be a very large agency which offsets its overheads against a very high turnover and can therefore slash its margins. It may even be trying to get into this organization, this market or this sector, and using this contract as a kind of 'loss leader' to get its foot in the door.

- Agency B may be charging more. It may have a better reputation for quality and the client may be willing to pay more for a contractor from Agency B. Little does the client know that both agencies have access to an almost identical list of contractors.

And I can't be the only contractor who has had the experience of an agency ringing up, offering a contract 'for which we are the preferred supplier' when you have already been offered a higher rate for doing the same contract, by another supplier.

How can this situation arise? Easily – because clients often have several preferred suppliers. A small slip of the tongue (let's be charitable) on the part of the recruitment consultant turns *a* preferred supplier into *the* preferred supplier, which gives quite a different impression; if you didn't know better it would imply that only this agency can get you the contract as it is not available elsewhere. Not of course, that the recruitment consultant is in any way seeking to give that impression.

The Interview

This is not the place to give you detailed information on how to conduct yourself at interviews – that is a matter of your professional expertise in your own industry. But there are a couple of things to watch for. One is that, unbeknownst to you, you may be being interviewed by a contractor: contract managers are a growth area. So don't be critical of the agency – the interviewer could well be working through them.

There is one thing which contractors attending interviews should bear in mind, and that is punctuality.

Contractors must be punctual

Some organizations have had bad experiences with contractors arriving late, working the hours they choose to work and generally being a pain. As a contractor you have to be more professional, more punctual, pleasanter and harder working than permanent employees. It is especially important to arrive on time for the interview – but many contractors turn up a good half-hour early. Why? Because nearly all buildings now have a security policy which means that you have to queue up at reception and be issued with a visitor's pass before the security staff will phone up and tell your interviewer that you've arrived.

At busy times – first thing in the morning and after lunch – there will be lots of people trying to get into the building for meetings and interviews. You can arrive at ten to two for a two o'clock interview and not get processed until five past. The interviewer thinks you were late, even though you actually arrived in plenty of time. So get to reception a good 15 minutes before you need to. If you do get processed very promptly, you can always tell security that you are early and ask them to phone your contact in 10 minutes time.

The agency should brief you in advance about the contract, to give you the best possible chance of succeeding. It should also send you clear directions for getting to the interview, including the following information:

- The organization's name

- A detailed address

- The telephone number

- Who you will be meeting and that person's extension number

- The time of the interview

- A map, if relevant

If you have fax or email this can be sent instantly – otherwise it's a case of waiting for snail mail to deliver it.

Afterwards the agency will want to know as soon as possible – preferably as soon as you leave the interview – how it went and whether you are interested in the contract if you get an offer. This is so that they are well prepared to deal with the client and with other contractors they may have sent to be interviewed for the same contract.

What the agency should never do is to negotiate a rate, send you for interview, offer you the contract, and then reduce the rate. But this has happened to my knowledge – a client has forced the price down and the agency has passed on the full cut to the contractor. Agencies that behave like this are not worth bothering with.

ACTION LIST
Contract-
seeking

- You register with the agency

- Your CV is processed

- You are added to the agency's database

- The agency phones and asks to send your CV to a client

- You discuss the type of work and the rate you want

- The CV goes off

- The client requests an interview

- The agency sends you details of the interview and briefs you

- You are interviewed by the client

- You phone the agency with feedback from the interview
- You get an offer
- Final negotiations
- You accept the offer
- The start date is set
- Written contracts are exchanged.

Incredibly enough, when everyone wants to get things moving, this whole process has been known to be completed in a day. When people say that the contract world is fast-moving, they mean it.

5 Getting Paid

So – you've marketed yourself successfully and got a contract. Now comes the nice bit – getting paid. At this point it is probably useful to remind ourselves about the different kinds of contract work that exist, as summarized at the beginning of Chapter 2:

1. A 'supply of services' contract via an agency.

2. A direct arrangement with the client in which you are self-employed and invoice the client.

3. PAYE contracting through an agency – you work on contract, but you are not self-employed, i.e. you are an employee of the agency.

4. PAYE contracts, i.e. short-term contracts in which the client pays you as an employee.

5. Non-agency third-party arrangements – you work freelance, for example for a production company which is in turn contracted to a TV company.

In this chapter we are going to concentrate broadly on contractors whose work falls into categories 1, 2 and 5. There is very little advantage to anyone in being a PAYE contractor as in 3 and 4, except in the very short term.

How You Can Operate

When it comes to how you trade as a contractor, your choice is between:

- Schedule D self-employed
- One-person limited company
- Umbrella company
- A mixture of these

Sometimes you do not have a choice – the agencies in your field insist that you trade as a limited company. When this happens it is usually because the agency has you on a longish contract or is using you for one contract after another. An obscure clause in the Taxes Act means that the DSS and Inland Revenue might argue that the agency has been employing you.

If they successfully argued this, the agency would be liable for all the tax and PAYE it *should* have collected. Since it is unlikely that you would be the only contractor on its books that this applied to, it would probably sink the agency. So the agency insists that you trade with it as a limited company and therefore make your own PAYE arrangements.

Other agencies, however, are happy to use self-employed people. The fact that there is so much variation and confusion is another demonstration of the shambles that is steadily developing in the employment market-place as the UK government and institutions fail to keep pace with changes in employment patterns.

If you have a choice in how you trade, the following sections may prove useful in helping you to make a decision about which method is best for you.

Schedule D/Self-employed/Sole Trader

In some ways this is the simplest option. In theory you do not need a separate business bank account, headed paper, an accountant or even a name for the business. The practice, needless to say, is rather different.

This kind of trading is often called 'Schedule D'. Schedule D is the tax schedule you operate under which sets out what business expenses you can claim and so on. You do not have to be self-employed to operate as Schedule D – you can have a full-time job and have Schedule D earnings from freelance work as well. However, if you have any earnings from business activities you *must* register under Schedule D and inform your tax office that you have started a business. There are penalties for failing to do this within certain time limits. You will be given a Schedule D number, which you need to file in your business file, because agencies that allow you to trade as a self-employed person often ask for your Schedule D number.

Unfortunately you cannot just declare yourself to be self-employed. The DSS has to agree that you are, and in certain cases it has fought test cases against freelances/contractors to prove that they were not truly self-employed and thus disqualify whole groups of workers from registering as self-employed.

If you want to register as self-employed you should first check DSS leaflet IR56/NI 39, 'Employed or self-employed?' When you register as self-employed you will have to answer questions on the application form about the nature of your employment. Your accountant (I know you don't need one *theoretically*, but we'll come to that later) should be able to advise you. Key tests for self-employment used by the DSS are:

- Do you have a number of clients? In other words, do you work for a number of different people in the course of a year? If you can answer yes, you get a brownie point.

- If things go wrong, do you have to set them right at your own expense? Employees usually correct mistakes in the firm's time, self-employed people do not.

- Do you have to provide your own equipment?

There are other criteria, but as with so much employment regulation, DSS attitudes vary across the country and they sometimes seem to target certain industries for special investigation.

National Insurance for the Self-employed

Suppose that you have rung the DSS and got a form to enable you to register as self-employed. What do you have to pay?

Most self-employed people pay Class 2 National Insurance contributions. You can pay these by monthly direct debit or by quarterly bill. Frankly, Class 2 National Insurance is something of a rip-off: you get almost nothing for paying the contributions. For example, they do not entitle you to Unemployment Benefit; if you are pregnant they do not entitle you to Statutory Maternity Pay – you get the miserly Maternity Allowance instead – and so on. Quite why self-employed people should be penalized in this way when they are frequently paying far more National Insurance than many employed people is mystifying.

Self-employed people are not eligible for SERPS (State Earnings-related Pension Scheme) either (i.e. you will only get the basic state pension when you retire). So you really should make some extra provision for your pension – you can deduct pension contributions from your income before tax, so it is well worth doing.

There is more bad news. Some self-employed people also pay Class 4 National Insurance contributions because their income is over a certain level. Class 4 contributions are nothing more than an extra income tax – they are even paid direct to the Inland Revenue along with your income tax. One way to minimize Class 4 contributions is to register as a limited company – an option we examine later in this chapter.

If you are *really* unlucky and are mostly self-employed but do the occasional PAYE contract, you can find yourself paying Class 1, 2 and 4 National Insurance contributions.

Bookkeeping for the Self-employed

One of the pluses for you of trading as a self-employed contractor is that you can adopt a reasonably informal approach to running your business. However, unless you are an extremely strong-willed and self-disciplined person, this informality can gradually turn into total chaos. You don't have to do your accounts more than once a year (unless you are VAT registered), so guess what? Most sole traders forget about them until the end of the year and are then faced with a massive sorting out job which probably coincides with working on a project 200 miles from home: not easy. If you are self-employed, don't leave everything until the last minute. Set up at least a basic system in advance by following the steps below.

Step 1: Invoicing File and Summary
Put a copy of each invoice, numbered in sequence, into an invoicing file. Keep a summary sheet at the front of the file which lists the invoices that you have issued and which has a running total of your income so far this year. That way, at any time you can do a

rough and ready calculation of how much tax you owe.

(The way in which tax for self-employed people is administered is currently in transition and is changing to a scheme called 'self-assessment'. This is supposed to be so simple that you, the contractor, can work out your own tax and simply send a cheque to the Inland Revenue. As currently constituted, however, it is shaping up to be the biggest bonanza of all time for accountants specializing in private client business. The 1997 edition of this Yearbook will cover self-assessment and its workings in more detail.)

One thing that self-employed people are often confused about is the distinction between profit and income. It is important to realize that these two entities, though related, are separate. The money generated by invoices you issue is *not* your income. The *profit* made by your contract-working business, after deduction of expenses, forms part of your income, along with any interest, dividends or other income sources, but minus any pension contributions you choose to make. So filing your business accounts with the Inland Revenue is not the same as making a tax return.

Step 2: Expenses Grid and Receipts Envelopes
Most professional contractors will collect an assortment of bills, receipts and tickets. Your business expenses need to be documented so that if necessary the Tax Inspector can say, 'You spent £189 on stationery in January; can I see the receipts please?', and you will be able to supply the information.

A simple way to organize this is to fix on half a dozen expense categories that are relevant to you. What constitutes a legitimate business expense for a contractor will vary from one profession to another; the main distinction you need to make is equipment purchases, since these cannot be claimed directly but have to be depreciated over several years. If you are using an accountant, enter equipment separately and the accountant will work out the depreciation that can be claimed. If you are not, you need to consult a detailed guide to tax rules for the self-employed.

Get 12 envelopes and label one for each month of the year. Each month, get out that month's envelope and just stuff receipts in as you get them. That way, they are automatically date sorted at the year end.

Now draw up a grid with months along the top and your expense categories down the side. Use lunch hours, travelling time and 'waiting for a new contract time' to go through the envelopes as you fill them up, and enter the expenses against the grid. This way, when you get to the end of the year, your accounts are three-quarters done.

Step 3: End of Year Summary
At the end of the year, add a 13th column to your grid and use it to add up whole year totals for each of the expense categories. You now have an expenses total and an invoice total.

Step 4: The Difficult Bit
Now save yourself a lot of hassle and hand your accounts over to an accountant. Steps 1–3 are the easy bit. The difficult bits are working out capital depreciation, especially year on year; working out what can be claimed for the use of an office at home; working out what percentage of car use is reclaimable; what percentage of car purchase loans can be reclaimed; whether your pension qualifies for tax relief and so on. Unless you want to plunge in and become a tax expert in your spare time (if this seems an attractive option it may be time to think seriously about getting a life), I would strongly recommend that you get to Step 3 and then employ a professional.

The preparation of final accounts and the completion of an income tax return do not cost much as long as you have done all the donkey work first. The accountant will prepare the final accounts (probably just a summary sheet) then get you to sign two copies of them. One copy is for your records, and the accountant sends the other copy to the Inland Revenue. The accountant then fills in your tax return, showing your business profit as part or all of your income, and sends that off to the Inland Revenue.

At this point, the accountant will tell you how much tax you can expect to pay. This is useful in two ways. First, it alerts you to how much you need to have ready and when. Secondly, it allows you to check the demand from the Inland Revenue against the accountant's estimate. This process will change slightly under self-assessment, but since outstanding amounts will be settled once the business accounts are in, you will still need to check that the Inland Revenue's final assessment does not vary drastically from the accountant's.

(Another good reason for using an accountant is that there are obscure tax advantages in the date you choose as the set-up date for your business. Again, only an accountant can give you individual advice on this.)

If you've never used an accountant before, there are a couple of things you should be aware of – read the section later in this chapter called 'Choosing an Accountant'.

Bank Accounts for Self-employed People

As a self-employed contractor you really don't need a business bank account, although the bank, for obvious reasons, may be keen for you to have one. The number of business-related debits and credits going through your account will be very low. For most contractors there are weekly or monthly BACS payments from the agency and cheques drawn for incidental expenses. There is no reason why you cannot put these transactions through your current account and save yourself the expense of running a business account. After all, banks don't force employees to have business accounts, do they?

However, some sole traders do choose to set up business accounts because they choose to keep their business finances completely separate from their personal finances. Whichever you decide to do, you *must* keep all bank, credit card and building society statements, in case the Inland Revenue ever asks to see them.

Nicolette, a contract trainer, didn't – and here's what happened to her:

When I first started contract-working I was self-employed and I took good care to do the business accounts properly. I didn't have a business account – BACS payments went into my current account and cheques went into the building society. I never particularly bothered to keep my bank statements because it never crossed my mind that I could possibly be involved in tax investigation. I had no undeclared income, I paid tax, I was completely honest in the way I ran the business, so why investigate me? But that's what happened – to this day I don't know why.

The results of the investigation were OK, as I knew they would be. In fact, I even made a profit on it because the Inspector found two part-invoices that didn't show up on my bank account. At first he made it clear that he was sure I'd salted the money away somewhere. In fact, the client had never paid them and I'd overlooked them. So the client belatedly paid me. But in the year they were investigating I'd only kept about half my bank statements and the cost of getting replacements to show the Tax Inspector was £5 a sheet. Now I keep everything.

The moral of this tale is – if you are self-employed never throw anything away. And don't assume that being honest is enough to keep you on the right side of the tax authorities – it isn't, so proceed on the basis that if you *are* ever investigated you can produce every piece of paper the Inspector asks for.

ACTION LIST
Self-employment

- Tell the tax office that you have started a business.
- Get a Schedule D number.
- Set up National Insurance payments to the DSS.
- Get an accountant.
- Set up a bookkeeping system.
- Keep all statements.

Trading as a Limited Company

There are definite advantages to trading as a limited company, so don't be put off by the fact that it sounds slightly 'high finance'. It's not much more complicated than being self-employed, and the complex parts (such as working out PAYE) can be cheaply handled by an accountant or bookkeeper.

Setting up a Company

Contractors usually buy an off-the shelf company. This is a company with a basic structure. You can buy a company that existed previously, in which case you will have to live with the name that the company was given, or for a few pounds more you can choose your own name. When you choose a name, you (or your accountant) has to check that the name does not already belong to another company. If it does you may still be able to use it if the other company is operating in an entirely different field – but you may have to choose another name.

You also have to choose a company secretary, and this must be someone you trust, particularly if you allow them to be a co-signatory on the cheque-book. A lot of contractors choose their partner or a parent. The forms now go back to Companies House and after a couple of weeks you get your company registration kit, which includes:

- *Memorandum and Articles of Association*
  These say what kind of company you have bought.

- *Certificate of Incorporation*
  This sounds impressive, but is in fact a flimsy thing which any half-competent Desk Top Publishing (DTP) operator could knock up on a PC in half an hour. But keep it carefully – you will need this in order to set up a bank or building society account for the company.

- *Share Certificates*
  There will be as many share certificates as you have issued shares – at the very least, one for you and one for the secretary. Some contractors like to issue more shares to themselves than to any other shareholder, just in case of divorce, disagreement or other unforeseen circumstances.

Incredibly, Companies House does not send you any information on *how* to run a limited company. This is despite the fact that there a lot of formal procedures that you have to follow – what are you supposed to do, guess?

Invoicing as a Limited Company

You will need headed paper – these days you can use a PC to design it yourself, but if the company's image is important, take it to a graphic artist for a customized design. You should include details of the company's registered office, its number (on the Certificate of Incorporation) and the Directors' names.

If you are registering for VAT, you need to get a VAT number issued to you *before* you start adding VAT to invoices. See Chapter 6 on VAT for details.

Setting up an Account

You will need a separate bank or building society account and a company cheque-book. As a contractor, your business account operates rather differently from someone running a conventional small business, such as a shop. You are likely to have a very low number of transactions on the account because on a given contract you are probably paid once a month and write no more than half a dozen company cheques a month (for salary, expenses and so on). The best bet for you is, therefore, to choose an account in which the charging structure fits well with a contractor's business pattern.

A building society account which might suit contractors is the Nationwide Business Investor account. The snag is that you need £2000 to open it. The benefits are excellent and it is an account that is particularly suitable to the level of monthly financial transactions that most contractors are likely to have. It pays interest, and you can write up to six cheques a month absolutely free. For a lot of contractors that is all they need. Agencies can pay by BACS into the account. The charges after the first six items are £2 per withdrawal – a lot more than a bank, so you need to weigh up whether you're likely to write more than half a dozen business cheques a month – most contractors don't.

If you can stick to the limits, this has to be the cheapest way for a contractor to operate a business account, provided you have that initial £2000. Phone the Nationwide on 0800 302010 and they will send you an information pack and tell you what the current interest rates and charges are.

However, there are a couple of reasons why a building society account may not be the best choice for you. If you think that you are going to need an overdraft, you may be better off with a bank because a bank can be more flexible. When you first set up a company you may well do so in a hurry – for instance if you have previously been self-employed and an agency has insisted you trade as a limited company in order to get a specific contract. In this case, you can find money being paid into your limited company account which is hard to draw out.

Obviously, you could pay yourself a large salary, but this increases tax and National Insurance costs and rather defeats the object of trading as a company. So, you may find your current account plunging into the red while your company account is firmly in credit. Clearly, if both accounts are at the same branch and you explain the situation to your account manager, he or she can see that you have assets to clear the overdraft and is likely to take a sympathetic line. If the business account containing the money is elsewhere, the bank will naturally be more cautious.

Some contractors reduce the costs of running a limited company by getting together with a trusted friend who is also a contractor and jointly running a company.

Umbrella Companies   Alternatively, you can trade through an umbrella company. This can be a good choice if you are trying out contracting and are not sure whether it is what you want to do long-term. It may also be suitable if you were previously self-employed or PAYE and are not sure whether you want to trade as a limited company.

The basic idea is that an accountant runs a company on behalf of a number of contractors and the umbrella company takes over the contract with the agency. The agency invoices the client for each contractor and the contractor receives some pay each week or month on a PAYE basis – note that you will have to pay both employer's and employee's National Insurance. The contractor then draws the rest of the income he or she has earned through dividends. Most umbrella companies also have mechanisms for you to draw expenses from the company.

This is not a cheaper option than having your own limited company run by an accountant, but it does enormously reduce the amount of paperwork that you have to do, so if, for example, you are a parent who is also working full-time, time may be more precious to you than money and you may find the slightly higher fees well worth it in terms of the time-saving benefits. It is important to find a reputable umbrella company – check with fellow contractors and find out how long the company has been trading, how contractor's money is safeguarded and how many contractors it has on its books.

No Other Cheques!

There are only three ways to get money out of your company account:

- Salary

- Expenses

- Dividends

You must not write yourself a cheque unless it is tied to one of these. If you do, the Inland Revenue is likely to classify the payment as a loan from the company to you.

Paying Yourself a Salary

When you set up a limited company, you become an employee, in fact probably the only employee, of the company you own. At first this doesn't sound like much of an advantage, but remember that when you own your company you are also the employer. It is the combination of these two roles that can be advantageous. As long as you stay on the right side of the regulations, you can set yourself up as a dream employer, lavishing benefits upon yourself as an employee, such as the maximum car mileage payments allowed by the Inland Revenue.

You can also set the level of salary that the company should pay you each month. Many contractors set this level as low as possible – the more daring ones set it at the level of the personal tax-free allowance. The reason that they do this is that salary attracts National Insurance Class 1 and 4 payments, on a sliding scale. The lower your salary, the less extra National Insurance you have to pay (confirming once again that National Insurance is in fact just another tax).

However, as long as you are paying employee's National Insurance contributions and your company is paying the related employer's National Insurance contributions you are building up an employed person's National Insurance record, which entitles you to much better welfare state benefits than a self-employed person. The fact that the self-employed person is probably paying much more in National Insurance only goes to highlight the inconsistencies of the current system. If you are self-employed, the government does not pay into SERPS (the State Earnings-related Pension Scheme). If you are employed and contracted into SERPS, the government contributes – but remember that the amount is proportional to the amount you are paying yourself, so you have to balance lower National Insurance contributions against lower government SERPS payments.

So being an employee can have its advantages. But it also has drawbacks. If you have a company car, it becomes a taxable perk, which is not the case for self-employed people. Many company-based contractors now choose not to have a company car and instead claim a mileage allowance for business travel. The Inland Revenue limits for this are fairly generous – at the time of writing they are 43p a mile for the first 4000 miles and 29p a mile after that – enough to cover modest running costs.

Most accountants offer a PAYE service for a modest monthly fee. You tell the accountant how much gross salary you want to pay yourself. Although you retain your own money in your company bank account, each month the accountant runs a payroll for you and produces a slip showing these totals:

- Salary this month

- Tax due on the salary

- Employer's National Insurance

- Employee's National Insurance

You can use these slips to keep a record of how much tax and National Insurance you will need to pay each quarter.

Paying Yourself Expenses

You can claim any *legitimate* business expenses from your company account. Draw up a weekly or monthly expense summary, fill it in, clip the relevant receipts to it and file it. You can then write yourself a company cheque for the relevant amount.

Paying Dividends

So how do contractors get the money out of the company? They wait until some profits have built up in the company account, then they declare a dividend. The tax on dividends is paid by the company, not by you as an individual. The rate was set by the Chancellor of the Exchequer, Kenneth Clarke, at 24p in the November 1995 budget, the same as the standard rate of income tax. Dividends don't attract extra National Insurance, so this is a very tax-effective way for contractors to pay themselves.

However, you must be careful and should bear the following health warning in mind. The Inland Revenue is not mocked, and it takes a dim view of the practice of paying yourself almost no salary and taking nearly all your pay as dividends. There is nothing illegal about it – they just don't like it – so you have been warned. The other thing that the Inland Revenue does not like is contractors who pay dividends over-frequently. They would argue in these cases that the contractor is taking dividends as a form of salary. In fact – let's face it – the Inland Revenue is generally uncomfortable with one-person limited companies.

As contractors, we may find this a bit rich, given that it is the Inland Revenue's own legislation and practices that force us into trading as limited companies in the first place. This area is almost bound to attract some kind of legislation in the future. Bear in mind, too, that a change of government usually heralds a whole lot of changes to tax arrangements. This is where the professional contractors' press is so useful – you will find articles written by accountants which explain the implications of any changes for contractors.

Before you pay a dividend, you have to hold a meeting, attended by the company secretary and properly minuted, to declare the dividend. Next, you tell the accountant how much you want to pay and the accountant produces a tax voucher for the shares in your company. This shows the shareholders' names, the number of shares, the dividend and the tax credit (i.e. the amount of tax the company must pay on the dividend). This is 20% at the time the dividend is declared – the remaining 4% is paid later, so remember to set both amounts aside. The company secretary has to sign the tax voucher and you then return it to the accountant for final processing.

Bookkeeping

The bookkeeping and accountancy side of running a company is more expensive than the self-employed equivalent. If the turnover of the company is under £95 000 at current rates, it does not need to be formally audited. But you are strongly advised to get an accountant.

Software packages which can help

There are a number of accounts and bookkeeping software packages that can help you keep records. Many contractors use a simple spreadsheet package, but for those who use a purpose-built package the most popular choice is probably QuickBooks from Intuit software. It costs approximately £108 – you can check the exact price by ringing the freephone number listed below.

Jon Vogler reviewed QuickBooks in the March 1995 edition of *Computer Contractor*. One of the points he made about it is that when using QuickBooks the average contractor can 'forget all the sacred jargon of the accounting profession: "nominal ledgers", "double entries", "postings" and, worst of all "debits" and "credits". QuickBooks uses simple expressions like "customer list", "receive payment", "deposit cheque" and "pay bill". This does not mean the accounting structures are weak. The ledgers and double entries are still there but they are... not obtrusive to the user'. He goes on to add 'There is excellent on-line Help..., 500 pages of documentation: well-written, grammatical and jargon-free..., excellent free telephone support, with advisors who know what they are about and short waiting times. Despite its US origins, QuickBooks has been thoroughly adapted to UK and EEC VAT, tax and accountancy practices... no transatlantic vestiges remain'.

You can contact Intuit for an information pack at this address, or use the freephone number:

Intuit
3 Manor Court
Harmondsworth
Middlesex
UB7 OAQ
Tel: 0800 585058

ACTION LIST
Setting up a
Limited
Company

- If you want an original name, think one up.

- Check with Companies House that the name is not already in use (your accountant can do this for you).

- Appoint a company secretary.

- Ask the accountant to form the limited company.

- Register for VAT if appropriate.

- Set a salary for yourself.

- When the registration certificate arrives, use it to open a company bank account.

- Set up bookkeeping mechanisms for recording:
    - Invoices issued
    - PAYE
    - NI
    - Salary
    - Expenses payments
    - Dividends

- Get headed paper which shows the registered office, directors and company registration number.

- See your accountant about car expenses, how to issue a dividend and what records to keep.

6 VAT and the Contractor

At the end of a meeting recently, the conversation turned to VAT. Someone remarked that the reason the police like to mount joint operations with the Customs and Excise Department is that VAT inspectors have much greater powers of search and entry than the police do. It may be as well to keep this sobering fact in mind as you read the section on VAT....

Should I be VAT-Registered?

I'm going to assume that most people reading this book are offering professional services and working either through agencies or directly for medium- and large-sized organizations. There are several things to consider when you look at whether you should be VAT-registered or not.

Let us look at the legal position first. There is a set turnover level above which you *must* register for VAT. Note that the word is *turnover*, not *profit*. In other words, the VAT threshold level is tied to the level of invoice income you receive, not the net profit you make after expenses. The threshold at the time of writing, set by Kenneth Clarke in the November 1995 budget is £47 000 per year. The Chancellor of the Exchequer reviews the amount regularly and raises it if it is felt that too many small businesses are being dragged into the VAT net.

For lots of firms which buy raw materials and market them to the general public this is crucial, because it effectively enables them to operate at a 17.5% discount. For you as a contractor, it is almost certainly irrelevant. If you are billing local or central government, educational institutions, the NHS, any but the smallest company, or any agency, the VAT from your invoice will be reclaimed by the organization that receives the invoice. In the jargon, your VAT output becomes their VAT input. They pay it then reclaim it.

So there is no net gain to the Exchequer. The money simply makes a merry journey from the account of the organization you invoice, to your bank account, to the Customs and Excise and then back out to the organization again when they reclaim the VAT they paid you. No tax is collected, but no doubt a good few hundred jobs are created to process all the payments. Quite why VAT payments and reclaims cannot be netted off in some way to prevent this waste of everyone's time is unclear to everyone except the Customs and Excise Department.

Even though you are not over the limit and do not *have* to be registered, you can still choose to be. Many people are under a misapprehension that if they are going to trade as a limited company, they will have to be VAT-registered – not so. The same threshold rules apply to both limited companies and to contractors trading as Schedule D self-employed. So should you choose to be VAT-registered? We have seen that charging VAT is not really relevant, since the organizations you are likely to be invoicing will simply reclaim it. The real reasons for being VAT-registered depend on what you have to spend in order to get a contract done. Let us look first at the benefits of being VAT-registered.

What are the
Benefits?
If you are VAT-registered, you can reclaim the VAT on anything you spend for business purposes. This sounds great, but needs some careful consideration. Many items that contractors spend money on are zero-rated. Let us take two examples:

- *Contractor A*
  Contractor A travels by train on a Monday morning from his home in Essex to Brighton. There he rents a flat during the week with two other contractors – it's cheaper than staying in a hotel or guest house. During the week they live on takeaways, buy the odd book to read and visit the cinema. Contractor A is making good use of his time in Brighton by taking a six month postgraduate course at Sussex University, which takes up two evenings a week.

- *Contractor B*
  Contractor B is working on the same project as Contractor A. She travels by car to Brighton from her home in Luton. During the week she stays in a small hotel and eats in the hotel. She is doing a remote learning course via the Internet, run by a management consultancy.

None of Contractor A's expenses attract VAT and therefore although he may be collecting VAT there is very little he can claim back in the way of business expenses. Assuming that the hotel and management consultancy are VAT-registered, everything Contractor B does carries VAT, which she can reclaim (although car expenses are a complicated subject, covered later in this chapter).

Obviously, there is no point in paying VAT just so you can reclaim it. And most people don't have a lot of choice about where they stay or study and how they travel. These case studies simply illustrate that the benefits of VAT registration are a matter of personal circumstances and preferences – how you as an individual contractor, operate. It is not possible to give advice that will be applicable to all contractors.

One definite benefit, however, of collecting VAT from your clients or agency is that you can keep the VAT in the bank or building society until you are due to pay it to the Customs and Excise – so you may make a little interest.

Cash Accounting

However, small amounts of interest can be more than offset by overdraft charges if you have to pay the VAT on an invoice you have issued before the client or agency pays the invoice. This situation arises because you normally have to account for VAT on invoices issued, not on invoices paid. This is less likely to happen with agencies, who tend to be fairly prompt payers, than it is with clients, who for various reasons may take a while to pay up.

But help is at hand for the beleaguered contractor, in the form of the cash accounting scheme. This scheme is intended to help small businesses (i.e. the average contractor) who would suffer cash-flow problems if they had to pay VAT on invoices that had yet to be paid. If your yearly turnover is, or is expected to be, under £300 000, you need only account to the Customs and Excise for VAT on invoices that have been paid in the relevant three-month period. In other words, you only pay the VAT you have actually collected and banked, not the VAT you expect to collect when an invoice is paid. What's more, you can deduct all the VAT on expenses you have paid during the period – which could mean that in your first trading period the Customs and Excise owe *you* money.

However, you cannot simply decide to opt for cash accounting. You must register the fact with Customs and Excise, using the form contained in VAT Notice 731 (a leaflet). Then Customs and Excise have to give you written permission to join the scheme. If you are registering for the first time, ask for the cash accounting form to be sent along with the rest of the registration information. And that brings us to how to register.

How to Register for VAT

Phone your local Customs and Excise office and tell them that you want to register for VAT. They will send you:

- *The VAT Guide (Notice 700)*
  This is the official Customs and Excise guide to VAT for businesses. Most of it is reasonably easy to follow, though there are parts that are slightly obscure. If there is anything you cannot understand, phone the local office and ask them to explain. Not surprisingly, they are used to fielding this kind of phone call. Realistically enough, the guide tells you that not all the information will apply to your business and not to bother reading the guide all the way through but to use the index at the back and look up what you need to know.

- *Notice 700 The VAT Guide – Supplement*
  There is a supplement to the VAT guide which adds extra regulations and is updated fairly regularly. You may also find the publications listed at the end of this chapter useful.

Claiming Expenses Once you are Registered

Let us start with cars, since a lot of contractors have one. You cannot reclaim the VAT on a new car, even if you are VAT-registered. You can reclaim the VAT on repairs and fuel, but it is not a simple matter of deducting the VAT you have paid. A system of scale charges applies in which you do not actually tot up the petrol you have used. You notify Customs and Excise of the size of your car and the mileage you expect to do and you then apply one of their scale charges.

Customs and Excise have explored the distinction between private and business motoring with enthusiasm and finesse. As a result, they make a number of points in the VAT guide about the distinction between these two kinds of car use. One of them in particular is one you'll come across elsewhere in this book. It is this:

> Travel between a person's home and normal workplace is private motoring. Travel from home to any other place for the purposes of business is a business journey.

This rule is also adopted on occasion by the Inland Revenue. Think about it. If you are a contractor you have probably read the paragraph above and decided that it does not apply to you. After all, you are not a permanent employee and you don't have a normal place of work. Every trip you make to the client's place of work is a business trip – isn't it?

Not as far as the VAT and some branches of the Inland Revenue are concerned. In fact, the Inland Revenue is currently fighting a contractor on this very point. (There are whole brigades of contractors out there, especially in IT and engineering, who like nothing better than a lengthy legal wrangle with officialdom.) The Inland Revenue is claiming that if you spend more than three days a week at a client site, that is your normal place of work. Never mind that you have a short-term contract and are paid not by the client but by an agency in a completely different location – this is your normal place of work. Clearly, as we shall see in the section on tax, this has implications for the expenses you can claim.

However, this rule does not seem to be being applied coherently across the whole of the UK. Nor is it generally applied to people trading as Schedule D self-employed, who are treated more leniently. The real targets seem to be the limited companies run by many contractors as invoicing vehicles. Yet the way the rules are interpreted also varies across the country. All the contractors I have spoken to claim travelling expenses from their companies for five days a week at a client site and have never been challenged. Perhaps they are all in for a nasty shock one day.

Be that as it may, Customs and Excise insist that this is private motoring. You cannot help wondering what they would say if you travelled to the photocopying shop near your place of work, parked, made one 10p photocopy of a receipt, then walked round the corner to work. Would the car part of the journey count as a business trip? It is a good wheeze, and no doubt some contractor somewhere is even now trying it. As I said in the introduction, most contractors are not really organization people – much less bureaucracy people.

The scale charges work like this:

Car's CC	Scale charges (£)	VAT (£)
Up to 1400	120	17.87
1401 to 2000	150	22.34
2001 to 3000	225	33.51

(If you are driving over 4500 miles a month, a reduced scale applies.)

And Now the Good News

Buried deep in the VAT booklet, and not exactly trumpeted by Customs and Excise, is some pretty good news for contractors. This is Paragraph 42: 'Vat paid on goods and services obtained before VAT registration'.

If you have paid VAT on goods or services bought for your business *before* you were VAT-registered, you can – in certain circumstances – reclaim it when you register. This might apply if you have been trading as a contractor for a while before you register for VAT, or if you have been doing freelance 'Schedule D' work in your spare time before becoming a full-time contractor. It is especially worthwhile if you have bought any large items, such as a PC, before you were VAT-registered. You could be looking at reclaiming several hundred pounds, all told, for expenses that you've already met. Free money? Not quite. There are, you will not be surprised to hear, a few regulations.

Reclaiming VAT on Goods Bought Previously

1. The goods must have been bought by the same person who is now registering for VAT (see the section later in this chapter if you have been trading as a sole trader and are now becoming VAT-registered as a limited company).

2. The goods must have been bought for the business that is now registered for VAT.

3. You still have the goods.

4. You make up a stock list, detailing the goods. This has to include:

   – a detailed description
   – the date bought

- the date disposed of (if this was after you registered for VAT. If it was before VAT-registration, the goods are not eligible anyway).

You cannot reclaim the VAT on goods you have consumed, such as fuel.

Reclaiming VAT on Services Bought Previously

These are the regulations that apply to reclaiming VAT on services:

1. The services were bought by the same person who is now registered for VAT (but see the section below on people who have subsequently become incorporated, i.e. begun trading as a limited company).

2. You bought the services for the business which you have now VAT-registered and they were *business* services.

3. You bought the services not more than six months before you became VAT-registered.

4. The services did not relate to goods you no longer have – for example, servicing on a PC which you sold before you became VAT-registered.

5. You make a list which includes:
   - a description of the service
   - the date you received the service
   - if the service relates to goods you got rid of after being VAT-registered (e.g. repairs on a PC sold *after* VAT registration) you must provide full details and dates).

Reclaiming VAT Now that you are Incorporated

If you bought the goods or services as an individual but are now incorporated – i.e. trading as a limited company – you can reclaim the VAT on goods and services in these circumstances:

1. The goods or services were supplied to the person who is now registered for VAT.

2. They were obtained by a person who became a member, officer or employee of the body (this means you, if you are a director and employee of your company).

3. The person was reimbursed for the full cost.

4. The person who bought them (i.e. you) was not VAT-registered at the time they were bought.

But be careful. To reclaim VAT in these circumstances you have to satisfy *all* of the criteria in the lists, not one or some. If you are in any doubt at all, contact your local VAT office and ask for guidance. It really is not worth messing with these guys: they're scary.

A Soirée at the VAT Office

I'd been doing quite well, though I was also having quite a lot of expenses and I had a kind of sneaky feeling that I was over the VAT limit, so I phoned the local VAT office from a client's phone (OK, I was a bit paranoid) and asked them what the limit was. For one thing, I hadn't realized they counted turnover, not profit, and I was way over. So I didn't know what to do. I made another phone call saying that I'd like to register. I filled in the form and sent it back and then they sent me a number.

They also sent me an invitation to an informal evening presentation for newly VAT-registered people. This wasn't really my idea of a hot evening out, but anyway. I didn't know anything about VAT so I went along. I don't know about informal – at the door there was someone with a list of the people they'd invited and their VAT numbers, and this person ticked you off. (I've been registered for a couple of years now and I've never had an inspection visit – I always wonder whether they're hassling the people who didn't show up first.)

Anyway, there was a talk, then questions, then coffee and a chance to chat to your friendly local VAT inspector; a bit like stroking a pit bull. In fact, I've got to say that the one that dealt with my area of work seemed very nice. The funny thing was, they had all these leaflets out on the table, like what to do if you've registered late. And I didn't dare pick one up in case the Inspector saw me and cottoned on. And I could see several other people in the same position, sort of eyeing the leaflets and grabbing one or two when they thought no one was looking.

The one practical thing I got out of the evening was the maths lesson – how to do the VAT sums. My accountant said she was willing to do the VAT for me, but I was wasting my money since it was only a matter of simple arithmetic and I should do it myself. Well I can tell you, it's not that simple. I started off taking 17.5% off the price of things like stationery supplies and then discovered that was all wrong.

Marie-Ange, Contract Graphic Designer

Doing the Sums   Marie-Ange is right. It's not that simple and she made the commonest mistake that contractors make when they are calculating the VAT they reclaim on business expenses, which just goes to prove how innumerate we contractors are. Let's look at an example and see where it all goes wrong.

Suppose, for the sake of argument, that you go and get some photocopying done. You are charged £2.35 including VAT. Clearly the job cost £2.00 and 17.5% VAT was added. You now want to reclaim the VAT you paid on the photocopying. Marie-Ange assumed that she needed to take the total price she'd paid and take off 17.5%. But look at the calculation that gives you:

$$235 \times 17.5\% = 41$$

Yet if you look back, the photocopying cost £2.00 and the VAT added was actually 35p, not 41p. What has gone wrong? The problem is in calculating 17.5% of the sum including VAT. Actually, you need to work out how much VAT was added in the first place. You do this by using a magic sum which changes each time the VAT rate changes, but is currently:

Full amount (including VAT) $\times 7 \div 47$
= amount before VAT was added

In our original example:

$$235p \times 7 \div 47 = 35$$

The right answer!

Now you might assume that this is so trivial that in most contractors' accounts the VAT office wouldn't even notice. But if you take a look at a VAT return form, you'll see that the total boxes on the form tell the Customs and Excise computer everything it needs to know about whether you are able to work VAT out correctly. And if you can't, even if the amount over-claimed is trivial, you are far more likely to get an early and detailed inspection from a VAT inspector.

ACTION LIST
VAT
Registration

- If your turnover is over £47 000 per year (threshold set in the November 1995 budget), you *must* register.

- Phone the local VAT office. Ask for:
  - a VAT-registration application form
  - a cash accounting form

- Fill in the forms and return them.

- Set up VAT bookkeeping mechanisms.

- Receive a VAT number and cash accounting permission from the VAT office, along with a date for your first VAT period and return.

- Add the VAT number to your stationery and invoices.

- Document VAT collected (output tax) and VAT paid (input tax).

- At the end of the VAT period, compile a VAT account and enter totals on VAT return.

- Open the next VAT period.

- Within one month, send the VAT return plus cheque to VAT payment centre.

VAT Publications

You can get any of these publications free by phoning your local Customs and Excise office. (Whether or not it's wise to phone up under your own name and ask for the misdeclaration penalty booklet is another matter.)

The VAT Guide (Notice 700)
Notice 700 The VAT Guide – Supplement

Should I be registered for VAT?
 Ref. No: 700/1A/93

Filling in your VAT return
 Ref. No: 700/12/93

The ins and outs of VAT
Ref. No: 700/15/95

Relief from VAT on bad debts
Ref. No: 700/18/91

Keeping records and accounts
Ref. No: 700/21/95

Visits by VAT Officers
Ref. No: 700/26/92

Late registration penalty
Ref. No: 700/41/95

Misdeclaration penalty
Ref. No: 700/42/93

How to correct errors you find on your VAT returns
Ref. No: 700/45/93

Cash accounting
Ref. No: 731 5/94
(This notice includes the application form for joining the cash accounting scheme.)

7 Looking After Yourself

When you work as a contractor, you leave the cosy world of sick leave, holiday pay and group medical insurance. Now you have to look after yourself. OK, you were expecting that and you are thinking about health insurance and a pension plan. But have you considered some of the less obvious impacts that contract-working can have on your life? Those are what we are going to look at in this chapter, starting with insurance.

Insurance

Motor Insurance

Most contractors, whether Schedule D or trading as limited companies, do not run a commercial vehicle. They run a private car which is used for personal business use. However, it is important that you tell your insurance company that you are using your car in this way, particularly if this situation is different from your circumstances when you took out the insurance. It is unlikely to result in a rise in premiums, but the insurance company will probably amend your policy to give you specific cover for personal business use. It is much better to sort this out in advance than to wait until you have a bump and then discover the insurance company will not pay because you were using your car for business purposes and had not told them.

House Contents Insurance

Even if you are a contractor who works on site most of the time, you probably have various kinds of office equipment at home. This might include:

- Filing cabinet
- Calculator
- Fax machine
- PC
- Answerphone
- Stationery

If you are broken into and your PC is stolen (or the chips are removed from it), you may well get a very dusty answer from your insurers when you try to make a claim. They may tell you that you have been running a business from home and that you should have made separate provision for your business equipment, since it is not covered by a home contents policy. And there's more. They may claim that the fact you have been running a business from home invalidates your home contents insurance. While this may seem unreasonable, you have to remember that the insurance company is insuring against the *risk* of goods being stolen, and if you are running a business in which lots of strangers come to the house and eye up your business equipment you may be more likely to be broken into. In other words, running the business increases the risk of a burglary at your house.

Most contractors do not, in fact, run that sort of business. Clients don't come to them, they go to clients. There is no added risk factor. But the insurance companies don't recognize this. So if you are intending to become a contractor, you should check with your insurance company how it will affect your existing contents policy and, if necessary, take on extra cover.

'Home and Business' Policies

Many contractors take out a specialized 'Home and Business' policy. There are not that many of these on the market, although the number available will presumably grow as contract work grows. These policies are not cheap, but on the other hand there is probably little point in paying into a cheaper policy which will not pay out when you get burgled. We cannot expect insurance companies to keep up with modish fads like contract work, so most Home and Business policies give us a whole lot of cover aimed at people running a hairdressing salon or garment business in their front room, whether we want it or not.

Most of the Home and Business policies include these 'extras':

- *Public indemnity insurance*
  You can see the insurers' point of view – if you are running a business from home, then you must necessarily have members of the public coming round and must want insurance against them tripping over the carpet, breaking their legs and suing you. Most contractors never have anyone connected with their work coming to the house. Still, this might be very handy if the telephone engineer falls through the window.

- *Employer's liability insurance*
  If you are trading as a limited company, you must, by law, have employer's liability insurance, even though you are the only employee of the company. The London and Edinburgh policy mentioned be-

low provides employer's liability insurance and pays legal costs if you are prosecuted under the Health and Safety at Work Act. If you are trading through an umbrella company, you should check the position.

Again, though, this is hardly relevant to most contractors, who only employ themselves. While the idea of you as employee suing yourself as employer for negligence sounds quite a good wheeze, I have a feeling that the insurance company would not actually let you do it. So this is more pointless cover that we have to pay for.

* *Business interruption*
This is a useful addition to the policy because it covers loss of income if you cannot carry on the business (subject it has to be said, to a number of exclusions).

The London and Edinburgh Insurance Company is one of the providers of this kind of insurance. You can get details from your broker; London and Edinburgh can be contacted on 01903 820820.

Insurance warning – limited company contractors

If you are insuring goods and equipment which were bought by your limited company, then the limited company, not you personally, must carry the insurance. Check with the insurer or your broker before taking out any policy which combines both home and business cover.

On the move

Since most contractors travel around quite a lot, it is especially worth checking how a policy deals with claims for business equipment lost while you were travelling – for example, mobile phones, laptop PCs, briefcases and so on.

Professional indemnity insurance

This insures you against any claim for damages resulting from your failure to carry out your work properly. Most agencies have their own professional indemnity insurance which covers them against legal action from clients as a result of a contractor's action. However, unless you are operating as a PAYE contractor, you are not an employee of the agency and are not covered by its insurance.

Contractors trading as limited companies can always liquidate the company and buy another one for their next contract, although this is hardly recommended practice. It also leaves you open on two fronts: the client may choose to sue you personally, and the agency's insurance company may choose to sue you. Even if you have done nothing wrong, or it turns out in the end that they cannot sue you, you are going to run up heavy legal bills dealing with the situation. So professional indemnity insurance is worthwhile. This is an extract from a special booklet on insurance for contractors issued by the IT agency CSS Trident:

> If in the course of your business or practice you provide advice, designs or specifications – services which are relied upon or acted upon by another party – you can be held responsible at law.

> From the legal standpoint the position with regard to the 'duty of care' is the same for any professional. If you offer a service in a specific area and set yourself up as a specialist you owe a 'duty of care' to anybody who might reasonably rely upon your service and advice over and above that owed by the ordinary man in the street.

Inland Revenue Investigation Insurance

You don't have to be involved in anything wrong to be investigated by the Inland Revenue. Simple matters such as getting your accounts in late can be enough to prompt a full investigation. Once such an investigation gets under way, you will find it an expensive business, particularly if you have to get your accountant to accompany you on a visit to the Tax Office (and you would be ill-advised to make such a visit without an accountant at your elbow). The cost of fighting off an investigation can run into hundreds of pounds. Some professional indemnity policies cover you against this eventuality, and you can also buy insurance which specifically covers you for costs incurred in dealing with an Inland Revenue investigation.

Cash Flow

A cash-flow analysis is supposed to give you an idea of your income and expenses over the next few months. Banks supply traditional cash-flow forms with their small business kits, but these are not really suitable for contractors, for the following reasons:

- The form usually shows a year's worth of entries. This is fine if you are selling ice cream and can predict that sales will be high in the summer and low in the winter. Contractors can only predict their income for the duration of the current project – often far less than a year.

- The form assumes that income is variable. Since contractors sell their skills at a set rate and have a signed contract confirming this, there is no 'estimation' element in their income projection. Contractors know *exactly* what their income will be for the duration of the project.

- The form assumes that expenses are variable. Contractors don't really tend to have peaks and troughs of expenditure –the cost of doing a contract tends to be pretty much the same week after week. No surprises there.

So the cash-flow form is not as informative to a contractor as it is to a small business person. Nevertheless, the banks like to see them – and if you are doing well you can enjoy watching your bank account fatten. If you are doing badly you will get an early alert that you are going to need an overdraft.

Choosing an Accountant

Of course, there are contractors who don't use accountants. If you are the sort of person who does your own conveyancing you may well also be the sort of person who feels able to grapple with the intricacies of the tax system. For anyone else, I would strongly recommend an accountant. But be warned: the word 'accountant' is used by people who are not chartered accountants. In fact, anyone can set up in business and call themselves an accountant. Some non-chartered accountants are highly competent – some are not. All of the contractors I know who have had bad experiences with accountants have been using non-chartered accountants.

In sectors such as IT, which has a very developed contract market-place, there are lots of specialist accounting firms which deal with contractors. It is a good idea to shop around and compare prices and services on offer. Cloke and Co. is one of the reputable firms of chartered accountants and registered auditors, offering a reasonably priced service to contractors, and their address is listed below. JSA describe themselves as 'The Contractors' Accountant' and their number is also given below. The best thing you can do in choosing an accountant is to ask people what their accountant is like and go for a personal recommendation.

Cloke and Co.
Warnford Court
Throgmorton Street
London
EC2N 2AT
Tel: 0171 638 8992
Fax: 0171 256 7892

JSA
Tel: 0800 252640

Pensions

There is really no substitute for sound financial advice tailored to your personal circumstances, and I am not going to try to tell you what kind of pension provision you should make. For self-employed people, the advice is to take out a personal pension. This is very tax-efficient, because you can contribute a percentage of your pre-tax income (the percentage varies with age). Talk to your accountant and pension provider about setting up a personal pension.

For contractors trading as limited companies the position is slightly more complicated. Most contractors who are doing this limit the amount of salary they pay themselves (since salary payments attract National Insurance contributions) and pay themselves via dividend payments.

When it comes to pension contributions therefore, they have a problem. The possible contribution is a set percentage of salary, according to age. But with such low salaries, contractors cannot contribute enough to build up a decent pension. The answer is the executive pension arrangement. In this arrangement, your limited company makes the contributions and claims relief for them against corporation tax. There is still some relationship to salary, but the levels are far higher and enable you to make a meaningful contribution to a pension fund. Get your accountant to work out the details for you.

Getting a Mortgage

Needless to say, the building societies have yet to wake up and get to grips with the fact that there are a bunch of highly skilled, well-paid people out there who do not have, do not want to have and never will have, permanent jobs. Perhaps at some point in the next century they will wake from their torpor and start offering housing finance which bears some relation to real people's working lives. Quite how they can whinge at the government for not kick starting the housing market when they themselves deny mortgages to some of the most employable and highly paid people in the workforce is something of a mystery.

However, help is at hand. *Freelance Informer* reported in January 1996 that an enterprising mortgage broker has set up in business specifically to help contractors get mortgages He is Julian Howes of Graduate and Professional Business Services, and if you get turned down by a building society on the spurious grounds that you are less able to pay a mortgage than the average permie in so-called 'secure' employment, you can contact Julian on 01452 770805.

Furthermore, there are some signs of movement. In February 1996 Allied Dunbar started advertising 'Mortgages especially for directors and the self-em-

ployed'. It seems that they have developed a mortgage package with a major bank, with a range of
repayment methods and no need for three years'
audited accounts. Sounds too good to be true? Well
Allied Dunbar is an insurance company, so you can
expect insurance to figure somewhere. However, it
may be worth giving them a ring. Contact the mortgage desk at Freedman and Co. on 01727 836511 (24
hours) or fax them on 01727 840976.

Insuring Your Health

Contractors tend to take far less time off sick than
permanent employees, for the obvious reason that
they don't get paid for it. If you're feeling slightly
queasy, the thought of how much it is going to cost
you to take a day off can make you feel downright
nauseous. Most contractors would rather be paid for
feeling ill, and tend to struggle to work armed with
quantities of Day Nurse and Nurofen Cold and Flu.
The one thing they dread is a really serious illness that
deprives them of income for weeks or months. For
this reason, contractors tend to think seriously about
health insurance.

There are two main kinds of health insurance you can
go for: permanent health insurance (PHI) or critical
illness cover. With PHI you pay a premium every
month, and if you are off sick you get a weekly
payment from the insurance company. As with all
insurance, PHI policies tend to have a great many
exclusion clauses and caveats, so it is essential to read
the small print carefully. You will have to write down
almost every illness you have ever had, and it is not
unusual for insurance companies which run PHI
schemes to turn down or restrict cover on the basis of
your medical history.

Because of this, many contractors opt for critical illness cover. With this kind of insurance, the policy specifically names a number of diseases and conditions – if you are diagnosed with one of them the company pays out. Again, read the small print. A survey in the January 1996 issue of *Money Management* magazine found that some critical illness policies have draconian restrictions and exemption clauses. An independent financial advisor is probably the best person to guide you through this minefield.

Let's face it: many contractors fail to do anything at all about pensions, health or anything else. The nature of the contract-working life can encourage a 'live for today' attitude where you never think beyond the end of the next contract. But try to think ahead – contractors in many industries have very lucrative careers but very short ones. Have a realistic idea of how long you can expect to work for. If there is no one in your office over 45 it is very unlikely that you will be the shining exception kept on until 55. Plan your finances accordingly and don't let any financial adviser talk you into making massive contributions over a very long period unless you are reasonably sure that you will be able to find contracts right throughout that period. It is pointless having a wonderful pension lined up for the age of 55 if you find that you cannot afford to contribute to it after the age of 45.

8 Developing Your Career

As we have seen at various stages in this book, when a client engages a contractor, the client is buying a set of skills, not a person. You, as a contractor, are expected to arrive on site fully trained and experienced; productive from day one. The cost of buying this expertise is factored into your day rate and is part of the reason that contractors are more expensive than permanent staff.

But if you are a long-term contractor, you begin to run into problems on the skills front. Most sectors are in a process of continual change. As a contractor, how do you keep up and keep your skills marketable? Clearly, to some extent, simply doing a contract keeps you up to date. But if new skills or working practices begin to be in demand, you can find that they attract a premium and rates for your existing skills begin to slip. Most contractors know that their skills are their most precious asset. They keep a sharp eye on how marketable they are, and when they see their skills beginning to go out of date, they have no option but to train themselves. In this chapter, we shall look at self-training.

Plan Your Own Career Development

There are several basic steps to take as you work out your personal career development plan:

- *Identify the opportunities that are available*
  Spend time thinking about the kind of contract work you want. Make a list of the skills, experience and qualifications you will need to get it.

- *Audit your own skills*
  Take stock of your own skills. Remember to include skills such as project management, finance management or self-management which you may have acquired in the course of carrying out contracts.

- *Carry out a training needs analysis on yourself*
  Look at the base skills that you have and the higher level or different skills you want. How big is the gap? Try to define precisely what kind of training you would need to have to achieve the skills you want. How long would it take you to migrate to the new skills? Are they wholly new skills or developments of skills you have already? Do they involve taking courses through professional bodies?

- *Assess the types of training available to achieve your goal*
  Rank them in terms of your personal preferences. The next sections describe the advantages and disadvantages of the various kinds of training available.

Face-to-face short courses

The advantage of face-to-face courses is that you have a trainer or lecturer present who can answer your questions. The disadvantages are that the quality of such courses is variable, they tend to be expensive and they go at the pace of the group, which may be faster or slower than you would ideally like to proceed.

To contractors, of course, time is money, and the cost of a course can be effectively doubled or trebled by the cost of taking time off work to attend it. The more entrepreneurial training companies have taken this on board and offer weekend residential courses and evening courses for contractors. (This is another good ground floor business opportunity, by the way. If this kind of service for contractors does not currently exist in your work sector, why not set it up?)

Agency Deals   A number of agencies are beginning to offer special training deals to contractors. These can take the form of training courses run by the agency itself or of negotiated discounts on training courses run by third-party training providers. If you think about it, it makes sense for the agencies to be involved in training. They are ideally placed to know what skills are in demand and what kind of training will impress the clients. And it is in the agency's interest to have well-trained contractors on its books.

Distance   Distance learning has developed hugely since the
Learning   days of the old 'correspondence schools'. The largest provider of distance learning in this country is probably the Open University, but with the advent of the Internet distance learning has taken on an entirely new dimension.

Colleges or specialist consultancies can download customized training packs to you; you can email the tutor with queries, engage in electronic group discussions with your fellow course-members, browse bulletin boards and forums to catch up with the latest professional developments and so on. There is no travelling and no geographical restriction. Even more conveniently for contractors, seminars don't even have to take place in 'real' time. They can be spread over the course of a week, as participants log on at a time convenient to them, read the contributions so far and add their comments to the ongoing debate.

Because you are no longer restricted by geography, you can buy your course from the market leader, even if its offices are at the other end of the country, and it can supply the course instantly. Furthermore, since the course provider does not need premises, printed course materials, equipment or a low staff to student ratio, the cost of the courses should be highly competitive.

European Study Centres

The idea of electronic teaching has now been adopted by the European Commission, which has sponsored the establishment of 40 European Study Centres across Europe. These provide graduate, postgraduate and professional level training and all the courses are delivered in English by universities participating in the scheme. The idea was described by Liz Heron in the *Independent on Sunday* of 15 January 1995. Britain has eight centres:

- Open University, London
- Open University, Newcastle
- Plymouth University
- de Montfort University
- Thames Valley University
- Sunderland University
- Anglia University
- East London University

Courses can consist of expert input delivered by satellite TV, on-line seminars, videoconferenced seminars and so on. The real advantage is the access it gives you to Europe-wide expertise. The disadvantage is that you presumably have to go into the centre to do the course. As you can see from the list, there is a fairly wide geographical spread in England, but no coverage in Wales, Scotland or Northern Ireland. The last time I looked these areas were also in the European Union, so quite why they have been missed out is not entirely clear.

Liz Heron writes:

> The European Open University Network... is developing an on-line information service on distance-learning courses offered by its five open universities and 150 traditional universities... new courses are being developed for the network that are designed to address specific skill shortages identified by the European Commission.

These developments are almost certainly just the beginning – there are bound to be further Europe-wide training developments as skilled people move around the EU in permanent or contract jobs.

Other Approaches to Training

More and more non-IT professionals are having to learn how to use pieces of software in order to do their jobs. Whether it's a spreadsheet, a word-processing package, a project management tool or a drawing package, the best way to learn it may be to buy it and load it on your PC at home. You can then train yourself – the manual will be useless for this, but bookshops are bursting at the seams with teach-yourself books, including the famous 'For Dummies' series. Alternatively, ask a friend who knows the package to give you 15 minutes of their time and do them a favour in return. When you are getting to know software, little and often is better than great chunks of training, because you retain more.

Is it
Tax-deductible? There is an Inland Revenue guidance note called 'Tax relief on vocational training' which sets out the position on whether you can deduct the cost of training yourself as a business expense. Basically, you can deduct the cost provided you have not claimed it already under some other heading – for example, if you are self-employed you must not have deducted it as an expense previously.

9 With One Eye on the Future...

Contract work is challenging the *status quo* in Britain right across the board. In this chapter there are two sections:

- A brief round-up of some British institutions and industries that need to recognize the enormous changes taking places in working patterns. No doubt you have your own favourites.

- A look at the global forces for change currently sweeping the international labour market, and some of the effects that they will have on workers in Britain and Europe.

Time for a Change

The Inland Revenue   At present taxation regulations for contract workers are illogical and seem to rest with the whims of individual tax inspectors. Perhaps we should call a halt to the long-running war between tax inspectors and the contract-working community and have published, nationally agreed guidelines on areas such as travelling expenses.

The NHS   By and large, most contractors I have spoken to are natural NHS supporters. A survey of contractors in *Freelance Informer* showed that the Labour Party was the most widely supported political party. But there is quite a marked feeling among contractors that I have spoken to that institutions like the NHS are unresponsive to their needs. Since the continuance of the NHS is dependent on its keeping the goodwill of the people who contribute towards it, some faint sign that the NHS is aware of the massive changes taking place in working practices would be welcome.

For example, in what way is the NHS 'free' to a contractor? If you have to give up a morning's work to wait to see your GP, you have lost half a day's pay. Effectively, you have paid that amount to see your GP. In fact, if you work it out you will probably find that for a routine visit it would be cheaper to pay the full cost of seeing your GP privately at a time that suits you. The service is only 'free' if you have a permanent employer who is willing to pay for your time while you hang around waiting to get seen, or if you are a traditional freelance who can organize your working day to suit yourself. Most contractors work on-site and are not paid for time off – they would be perfectly happy to spend their own time, in the evenings or at weekends, if the NHS would let them. It is losing pay during the week that they're unhappy about.

Banks and Building Societies   Lenders need to stop being scared of people without permanent jobs, and treat applicants on their earnings or earnings potential. Very few contractors want to take on enormous mortgages – most are very conservative about the income multiples they borrow.

The Holiday
Companies

The fortnight's holiday once a year suits permanent employees who can book the time off months in advance. But it doesn't suit contractors for several reasons. Firstly, and obviously, they don't get paid. And a fortnight without pay is quite a big chunk to take out of a month's earnings. A week is a lot easier to budget for and get over.

Secondly, contractors have a lot of trouble scheduling holidays. Clients are not usually happy for contractors to take a fortnight off in the middle of a contract. Some won't let contractors take any time off at all – it depends how urgent the project is.

The contractor is therefore left with two options. The first is to book the holiday in advance. Two weeks booked six months ahead is not a very good proposition because the contractor does not know where in the contract cycle he or she will be when the holiday falls due. If the contractor is just finishing a contract, two weeks is too long to be out of circulation because there is a lead time before the next contract can be arranged. Similarly, contractors looking for a new contract don't want to have to explain to the interviewer that they will be away for two weeks in the early stages – the interviewer is likely to choose someone else.

For all of these reasons, there are many contractors who limit their holidays to a week at a time – it's less disruptive. But by the same token, a contractor may have a confirmed start date two weeks from today and think, 'Great, just time for a week away in the sun!' – the second option. The contractor wants the holiday fixed up immediately. Also, the contractor frequently finds that he or she is the only person around who can take a holiday at such short notice – but is put off going alone by the idea of being a social outcast in the hotel.

So let's have more flexibility from the holiday companies, and less of the idea that you book in January for two weeks in August.

Forces for Change

Clearly, the Internet and the World-Wide Web will bring about profound changes and speed up the globalization of the labour market. The world-wide availability of skilled on-line labour will not affect those in the caring professions or those whose jobs depend on personal contact with people. But for millions of others, once the jobs market moves on-line we will see a weakening of the concept of a 'national workforce'. Let's look at why.

*Say 'Goodbye'
to the Green
Card*

It's all very well for the USA to impose immigration restrictions and a Green Card scheme. Suppose the worker does not physically have to enter the country in order to do the job? What price a Green Card scheme then? Is any American government going to be brave enough to bar American businesses from using the Web to pick up highly skilled labour who can log on from their own homes everyday? Particularly when these people won't have a 'job' in the way that people have had in the past, but will simply supply services, bill them and get paid by an on-line money transfer credit to their account.

*Say 'Hello' to
the Euro*

Think about the Europhobes, and their idea that highly skilled contractors will choose to stay in Britain to be paid in worthless Olde Englishe Poundes while the rest of Europe moves towards monetary union. Any contractor I know will be on the first Eurostar to Brussels or Paris to get paid in yummy Euros, which they will be able to exchange at an enormously profitable rate on their visits home. Britain will continue to be a pleasant place to live, but anyone mobile with skills will take good care not to get paid there.

Say 'No' to Government Bullying

The days when British governments could corral their populations within national boundaries are over. It isn't just business that's becoming global – so are workers. And if governments, whether Labour or Conservative, don't wake up to the fact they are going to have a nasty shock one day, when they find that a sizeable chunk of their skilled work force is earning its living elsewhere.

Don't Fear the Future

As contractors, we all work with one eye on the future, trying to anticipate what is going to happen in the workplace so that we are well placed to take advantage of it. Remember that an open mind and clear thinking can help you avoid the worst mistakes. Here is the kind of idiocy that technological ignorance and a light dusting of xenophobia can lead you into:

> In thirty years' time, although English will be the lingua franca, Japan's dominance will mean that English will be no more than the language of the global peasantry. The tongue – and the calligraphy – of the Elite will be Japanese.
>
> Sir Kenneth Clark, *Diaries*, December 1988

And here is the 1996 reality:

> Japan is thought of as a world leader in computer technology but when it comes to the Net, it is lagging behind

the US, UK and Germany. A table of Net hosts correlated with Gross National Product ranks Japan between Slovenia and Ecuador.

That gap – between Japan and its industrial competitors is becoming important... the obvious reason why the Japanese have not taken to the Net is the English language. More than 90 per cent of communications across the Net are in English. The Japanese find English difficult to learn and their own language is difficult to use on the Net. Nor are they widely computer literate: fewer than 10 per cent of offices are computerized, compared with 42 per cent in the US.

Richard Vadon, 'Drowning not surfing – net culture has intimidated Japan', *Financial Times*, 22 January 1996

Funny old world isn't it?

Tell us about your experiences as a contractor

That's it for 1996.

In 1997, *The Professional Contract Worker's Yearbook* will have special features on Europe and on how self-assessment of taxes is working out. Until then, happy contract-working. And remember that we are interested in what you have to say about contract-working in your industry – there's even a form on p. 199 to save you time if you have a comment to make.

PART 3

A View from the Industry

Interview with Luke Barnes – Contract Multimedia Designer

Luke Barnes is 44 and has spent the last eight years as the permanent employee of a multimedia company which both carries out its own projects and also supplies contractors to other companies. (Sometimes its permanent employees carry out contracts on the firm's behalf, but continue to be paid as permanent employees.) Luke recently decided to give up his permanent job and move over to become one of the company's agency contractors. I talked to him about his decision.

Why did you wait until now to become a contractor?
I suppose I was nervous really. I knew a lot of people who were permanent employees. I didn't have the nerve. I had a family, and as I was in a full-time job I just carried on doing it. My main fear was that I wouldn't get enough work as a contractor. What finally decided me was that I just wasn't earning enough to make ends meet as a permanent employee. Then the company I was working for had a financial crisis and I offered to become a contractor and take redundancy. Actually, at the same time I had been doing a bit of moonlighting as an off-site contractor, working from home. That's what really helped me to make the transition, otherwise I would never have been in a position to do it.

Why's that?
Because when you move into contract-working there's a dip in your income before you can invoice and get money in. As a permanent employee, I had no spare cash to cover this. But by moonlighting, I got enough cash together to go for it. That cash saw me through the first six weeks as a fully fledged contractor.

When you did finally become a contractor, why did you continue to work for the same firm?
They knew me and I knew they could offer me regular work. But at the same time, if someone else came along and offered me a more interesting or better paid contract, I could do it. So I had nothing to lose really.

How did you cope with the administrative side of becoming a contractor?
I spoke to another contractor and they recommended their accountant. The accountant ran through the things I needed to do, which I took notes on and then basically failed to do. He strongly recommended I set up as a limited company because there were aspects of my work situation that the Revenue had been suspicious about in other cases. His basic advice was to register as a company, write to the tax authorities, keep all my receipts and do as much of my own accounts preparation as I could.

Did you get a business bank account?
Well, I thought about getting one of these business building society accounts, but that wasn't actually any good because the Nationwide one I looked at required an initial deposit of £2000, which I didn't have. Anyway I forgot about it all for a while and work started coming in. Through a contact I got some work directly for a client; that's a continuing thing and I can fit that round the other contract work I get through the agency. I mean, my actual contract from the agency says I mustn't work for anyone else while I'm on contract with them. If I was feeling very asser-

tive, I'd strike that clause out of the contract before signing it, but at the moment I'm not quite sure enough of myself.

Has being a contractor changed your outlook?
After an initial period of anxiety, the anxiety continued unabated.

What's your state of mind now?
Well, on the one hand you think to yourself, 'If the work stops utterly, I've got to have so much put aside'. But then you also think, 'Well, to earn as much as I was earning as a permie, I've only got to work half the hours. So I'll go for a walk'. And these two states of mind alternate.

Did your age play a part in your anxiety about becoming a contractor?
I'm 44 and I knew that once I left my job, I'd never be employed as a permanent employee by a company again (unless it was as part of B&Q's 'employ the elderly' initiative). So there's a slightly chilling aspect that it's an irreversible decision – I can't step back into the supposed security of a job again.

I feel happier because I feel more in control of what I can do. I enjoy writing invoices. When I work for companies full-time I'm a moaner and now I work for myself I can't be. Also, I like the feeling that when I finally get arrested I can describe myself in court as a Company Director.

Also, it's nice when people ring up that it's now up to me where I am (I work off-site mostly). Plus the fact that I can organize my own time and I'm not 'nine to five' any more. Also, my former permanent employer is now much nicer to me. They want me to carry on working as a contractor for them and the contrast with their former attitude is chalk and cheese.

What about holidays?
Before I had a limit of 25 days; now I can take as much as I want, which is good because I've got children.

Have you made sickness and pension plans?
I don't like financial advisors. I was told to buy health insurance and take a pension payments holiday to pay for it. I now realize that the advisor was more interested in his commission than in giving me good advice. I feel a bit at sea with all this financial stuff and have a distaste even for reading about it.

How do you keep your skills up to date?
I feel that I'm going to need to train myself. Taking on new jobs means I have already learned new things. I'm going to get into new branches of multimedia. I'll do that by buying the equipment and software and teaching myself – I don't see myself going on courses because they're mostly crap. I think you can train yourself better than you can be taught on a course.

When will you stop work?
The thought of working for the next twenty years is very depressing. I'd like to develop into more interesting areas and that's easier when you're working contract. It gets more and more difficult as you get older to continually turn up in new offices and present yourself as a dynamic and fresh-faced contractor. You can't help wondering if they're thinking, 'Why is this person still doing this?' There's no career progression in contract work.

I caught up with Luke a couple of months later.

So how's it going?
Reasonably well.

Any surprises?
The delays in contracts starting – I didn't notice those when I was full-time. Projects don't start on time and

on average, I'm not fully employed every week – that's partly in the nature of working at home: it would be different if I was working on-site. I'm earning about the same but doing less work. There's a lot of stuff pending though, and I suspect it's all going to come in at once and there'll be a period of intense overwork.

Have you noticed any improvement compared with being a permie?
Not yet – but I still think I'm not yet into the routine. I think I'll get more organized and use my time more effectively.

What's it been like trading as a limited company?
So far only one invoice has actually gone into the limited company account. And I haven't managed to get any money out.

How are you going to deal with the problem of delays in contracts starting?
I'm not too worried as long as I'm earning enough. If it got bad I'd take on-site contracts or do more of a mixture of on- and off-site work.

What's your mental outlook been in the last three months?
Accidie, mostly.

Care to elaborate?
Not meeting people is a problem, because I'm working from home. The day can seem quite long. What I will be doing is trying to make sure I avoid this by developing some leisure activities. A contractor I know is learning Japanese, and I'll probably sign up for a course of some sort.

Have you got any regrets about becoming a contractor?
None. It's always the same old battle with oneself whether one's in permanent employment or contract-working.

PART 4

Industry Look-up

The pages which follow give an overview of how contract work operates in various industry sectors, and they also contain selective lists of agencies and relevant publications.

We welcome contact from agencies who would like to be included in the 1997 *Yearbook* (there is no charge for inclusion). Similarly, if you are a contractor with information about contract-working in your industry that you think might be of interest to other contractors, please get in touch. There are forms on pp. 199 and 202–3 that you can use. Complete these and send them to:

The Publisher, Trade and Professional
McGraw-Hill Publishing Company
Shoppenhangers Road
Maidenhead
Berkshire
SL6 2QL
Tel: 01628 23432
Fax: 01628 770224

Civil engineering, surveying, estimating and project management

As with other sectors, the construction industry recruitment consultants I spoke to described the new way firms were working – a core of permanent staff with contract staff to deal with any overload. Many firms in the construction industry work on a project basis, so they want contract staff to help achieve deadlines on a specific job, rather than to fill out their workforce. ('Contractor' has its own specialized meaning in this industry, so to prevent confusion I have tried to avoid the term.)

Contract professionals in the construction industry, as in other sectors, trade in a variety of ways – some are Schedule D, some operate as limited companies and some are PAYE.

An employment survey carried out jointly by Montrose and *Building* magazine in October 1995 reported on the trends for employing short-term staff contractors in the construction industry. The survey showed that 57% of contract staff earned more than they would in permanent employment. And more than half of the consultancies surveyed said that they would rather employ all contract staff, or a combination of contract staff and permanent staff. A quarter of the employers said there was friction between contract and permanent staff and 72% said that team spirit was harder to generate with staff on contract.

And staggeringly, nearly 40% of the employers had not calculated the relative costs of contract and permanent staff. When they do, they may be surprised just how expensive permanent staff are, even though contractors get paid more.

Publications

Building magazine
Tel: 0171 560 4141
Fax: 0171 560 4054

Contract Journal magazine
Tel: 01444 445566

Construction News
Tel: 01858 468888

Agencies

Many agencies have nationwide coverage. To find your nearest office, call the number listed and tell the operator which area you are in.

Albion Construction Recruitment
Westmead House
123 Westmead Road
Sutton
Surrey
SM1 4JH
Tel: 0181 770 1100
Albion handle site and project managers, quantity surveyors and estimators.

Euro Elite Consultants
Western Australia House
113–116 The Strand
London
WC2R 0AA
Tel: 0171 240 4440
Fax: 0171 739 7208
Email: recruit@euroelite.co.uk
Euro Elite supply professional contractors to work on building surveys, structural and urban design, CAD/Intergraph, public health and landscape architecture.

Hill McGlynn/Career Landmarks
6 Henrietta Street
London
WC2E 9PS
Tel: 0171 240 4433
Fax: 0171 240 2440
Hill McGlynn handle contract vacancies for estimators, site and civil engineers, quantity surveyors and project managers.

Leda Recruitment
Leda House
46/48 New York Street
Leeds
LS2 7DY
Tel: 0113 242 8090
Fax: 0113 242 9135
Leda supply estimators, site and civil engineers, and quantity surveyors.

Montrose Technical Recruitment
(part of the Hays Group)
Tel: 0171 828 4975
Montrose supply construction industry professionals for contracts nationwide.

Education

Agencies in this sector have to carry out police checks and List 99 checks on contractors. (List 99 is the list of teachers the Department of Education considers unfit to teach in schools.) Some agencies also carry out health checks before they register teachers.

There is huge growth in the number of education agencies – Select Education, which claims to be the biggest agency in Britain, will have 12 offices nationwide by the end of 1996. Katy Burns from the London office emphasized that as well as List 99 and police checks, Select Education insists that teachers are fully qualified and must produce the originals of their qualifications. All the agencies I surveyed in January/February 1996 were at their busiest period in the year and keen to get more teachers on their books. Most are quite open about their rates and many advertise them in the 'Agencies' section of the *Times Educational Supplement*.

However, the growth of agencies in the educational sector is not uncontroversial. In January 1996, Doug McAvoy, General Secretary of the NUT, wrote to teachers on the subject of teacher employment agencies and businesses in these terms:

> The development of agencies… is a direct challenge to the nationally determined salary scales and to the conditions of service applicable in schools throughout England and Wales.

The NUT's position is that agencies are undercutting directly employed teachers. In teaching and other industries where there are nationally agreed pay scales it is actually the contractors who are paid less, since the agencies have to cover their costs out of the standard day rate paid by the schools. Perhaps more realistically, the NUT has been in discussion with the Capstan agency (listed below). Capstan has agreed to pay the contract teachers it supplies at qualified teacher rates.

The NUT is focusing its current campaign on London 'where the problems are greatest'. This makes sense – after all, the opportunities to get work by registering with an agency that has London-wide coverage are greater. This issue looks like it will run and run. At its core are the complementary interests of two groups: permanent staff teachers and contract teachers. The NUT and the agencies are going to have to learn to live with each other. The issues are not simple, and we'll be reporting developments in the 1997 edition of the Yearbook. Meanwhile, if you are an agency teacher, we'd like to hear about your experiences of contract work in education.

Publications   *Times Educational Supplement*

Times Higher Educational Supplement

Agencies   Many agencies have nationwide coverage. To find your nearest office, call the number listed and tell the operator which area you are in.

1st Quality Supply
Tel: 0181 251 0094

Claims to be the longest established agency in the UK nationwide. Covers London, Surrey, Hampshire and Greater Manchester areas only.

ASA Education
Glade House
52 Carter Lane
London
EC4V 5EA
Tel: 0171 329 4777
Deals with primary, secondary and special needs teachers in London and the home counties.

Capstan Teachers
Meridian House
Royal Hill
London
SE10 8RT
Tel: 0181 293 5051
Capstan has offices all round the country and deals with nursery, primary and secondary teaching. The majority of its teachers are on PAYE.

Catalyst Education
Tel: 0181 518 8449
Deals with all areas of London – primary, secondary and SEN teachers.

Chalkface Recruitment Ltd
162d High Street
Hounslow
TW3 1BJ
Tel: 0181 570 1400
Deals with early years, primary and secondary teachers in North and West London.

Education Lecturing Services (ELS)
Tel: 0115 911 1199

Deals with lecturers. You can phone ELS to request an information pack and an application form for an entry on their database of lecturers.

HMS
Tel: 0171 636 7030
Specializes in the South London area and holds occasional open evenings.

LHR
222–224 Northfield Avenue
London
W13 9SJ
Tel: 0181 579 9899
Operates mostly in London.

Masterlock
Macmillan House
96 Kensington High Street
London
W8 4SG
Tel: 0171 938 1718
Deals with nursery, primary and secondary teachers in London and reports that the market is definitely growing.

Pro Tem
87 New Bond Street
London
W1Y 9LA
Tel: 0171 491 1045
Fax: 0171 629 1296
Deals with nursery, primary, secondary and special needs. Operates throughout London.

Reliance Education
Tel: 0171 404 3130
At the time the Yearbook *went to press, Reliance was offering a bonus for primary daily supply teachers. They specialize in London.*

Select Education Ltd
25 Euston Road
London
NW1 2SD
Tel: 0171 278 1666
*Has PAYE and 'limited company' contract teachers, but
no Schedule D. Teachers must be fully qualified. Deals
with nursery, primary and secondary education and is
about to move into further education.*

Teachers UK
Morgan House
249 Cranbrook Road
Ilford
IG1 4TG
Tel: 0181 252 5790
Fax: 0181 252 5105
*Very interested in primary school teachers across
London.*

Time Plan
Tel: 0181 343 4488
Deals with schools in London and Kent.

Executives – Interim Management

Interim management is one of the growth areas of professional contract-working. There is even an agency, Executives on Assignment, founded by Bob Snell, which is exclusively dedicated to providing top-quality temporary managers and executives. Executives on Assignment suggests six reasons why Chief Executives, Human Resources and other Directors might want to employ an interim manager:

- A key executive is leaving

- There is a temporary need to 'add weight' to the management team.

- The company may be missing out on business opportunities because of a shortage of the right kind of senior people.

- The company wants someone to implement some decisions without taking a permanent position.

- The company needs help with a change management plan such as an acquisition or disposal.

- The company is considering interim management as part of a review of the way it employs managers.

But be aware of some of the pressures of contract interim management. Writing in *Business Age* in December 1995, Bob Snell observed, 'It is a rare bird who has the attributes, the will power and flexibility to move jobs every three months and be effective from day one'.

Agencies   Many agencies have nationwide coverage. To find your nearest office, call the number listed and tell the operator which area you are in.

Executives on Assignment
Buckland House
Waterside Drive
Langley Business Park
Slough
SL3 6EZ
Tel: 01753 580582
Fax: 01753 580020

First Reserve
Holborn Tower
137 High Holborn
London
WC1V 6PW
Tel: 0171 404 6444
Fax: 0171 404 6933
First Reserve supplies interim management to the public sector nationwide.

Psec Consultancy Services
Psec plc
Fountain House
Great Cornow
Halesowen
West Midlands
B63 3BL
Tel: 0121 585 5701
Fax: 0121 585 6052

Psec offers consultancy and interim management across a range of health, local authority and community services nationwide.

Finance, Banking and Accountancy

Under the headline 'Banking on a temp job' in the *Evening Standard* of 20 February 1995, Michael Hanson summed up the reasons why banks, insurance companies and finance houses use so many contract staff:

> Apart from uncertain economic conditions there are other reasons why banks prefer to use temporary staff. In volatile sectors of the market, such as derivatives, foreign exchange or settlements, additional staff are often needed very quickly. They can also be dispensed with as soon as the heat is off.

In accountancy, the use of contract accountants has become commonplace. Hays Personnel Services reckons that the number of temporary accountants has grown at more than 30% for each of the past three years. Elizabeth Heathcote interviewed an accounting manager in a November issue of the *Independent*, who had this to say about contract accountants:

> I'm very pro the use of contract accountants. It gives me a fast result in response to increased need at heavy periods and an increased short-term resource.... Five years ago before the recession it was hard to get temps who were good enough. Now there are accountants who consider themselves to be permanent contractors, who like the flexibility. They're still a minority though. Most people are temping to keep money coming in between

jobs and are looking for something permanent. That's the way things are now.

I believe that hiring and firing is a thing of the past. If my requirement is anything short of two years, I will take someone on a contract.... I think short-term contracts are definitely the future. In fact, I think terms will become even more flexible.'

It's significant how often contractors across a wide range of industries cite 'dislike of office politics' as one of their main reasons for opting for a contract lifestyle. Harrison Willis, the recruitment consultants, carried out a survey which was reported by Roger Trapp in the *Independent*'s Graduate Plus section. It found that four out of ten accountants preferred contract-working to having a permanent job. Roger Trapp reports:

The 620 accountants working on a temporary basis with companies, the public sector and financial institutions cited a number of reasons – flexibility, variety, breadth of experience, paid overtime and the independence that comes from not being involved in office politics. About 40 per cent of the women polled found it allowed them to fit work in with their family commitments.

Many women (and quite a few men) find the incredibly long hours demanded by permanent career positions impossible to balance with the fact their children like to see them occasionally. Contract work, with its strictly defined working hours, can be a way out of this dilemma.

Publications   *Nine to Five*
Handed out free at London's main railway stations once a week. It contains lots of agency advertisements for temps and contractors in the financial world.

Money Marketing
Tel: 0171 287 5678

Post magazine
Tel: 0171 583 3030

Evening Standard 'Business Day' supplement

Agencies   Many agencies have nationwide coverage. To find
your nearest office, call the number listed and tell the
operator which area you are in.

Accountancy Personnel
1st Floor
7–8 North Street Quadrant
Brighton
BN1 3FA
*Accountancy Personnel is one of the largest firms in this
field – over 100 offices nationwide.*

Accountancy Solutions
25 Hanover Square
London
W1R 0DQ
Tel: 0171 499 7425
Fax: 0171 629 2170

Acme
Guild House
36/38 Fenchurch Street
London
EC3M 3DQ
Tel: 0171 929 5252
Fax: 0171 929 5364
Insurance and reinsurance positions.

Banking Personnel (Hays)
41/42 London Wall

London
EC2M 5TB
Tel: 0171 588 0781
Fax: 0171 256 5804
Back- and mid-office positions in the City, plus accountants for a range of roles.

Barbara Houghton Associates
City Business Centre
2 London Wall Buildings
London
EC2M 5PP
Tel: 0171 628 4200
Fax: 0171 972 9461
Specializes in contracts in settlements, reconciliation, loans administration, also TRAX, customer services, trade input, corporate actions and securities.

BGA Insurance Services
16 Devonshire Row
London
EC2M 4RH
Tel: 0171 377 2635
Fax: 0171 247 8430
Stop-loss administration; reinsurance technicians; accountants etc.

CSL Placements
Ashton House
Silbury Boulevard
Milton Keynes
MK9 2HG
Tel: 01908 848470
Fax: 01908 678941
Email: paul_vaughan@csl.touche.co.uk

Harrison Willis
Tel: 0171 629 4463
The recruitment firm quoted above, which surveyed contract accountants.

Hillman Saunders
Temporary Contract Division
78–79 Leadenhall Street
London
EC3A 3DH
Tel: 0171 929 0707
Fax: 0171 929 1666
Has ten years' experience in supplying insurance contractors.

InterSelection
14 Trinity Square
London
EC3N 4AA
Tel: 0171 680 0077
Fax: 0171 680 1052
Evenings/weekends: 0181 542 4075
A large agency which deals with a wide spread of finance, banking and accountancy contracts.

IPS Contract Management
Lloyd's Avenue House
6 Lloyd's Avenue
London
EC3N 3ES
Tel: 0171 481 8111
'Temporary Assignment Specialists to the insurance world.'

Joslin Rowe (contract banking recruitment consultants)
Court House
11 Blomfield Street
London
EC2M 7AY
Tel: 0171 638 0382
Fax: 0171 382 9417
Wide range of City and West End banking contracts

Joslin Rowe – Insurance Recruitment Consultants
Forum House
15–18 Lime Street
London
EC3M 7AP
Tel: 0171 283 6008
Fax: 0171 283 0690
Interested in contractors with one year's experience for a wide range of assignments.

Moore Wilshaw Associates
124 Middlesex Street
London
E1 7HY
Tel: 0171 247 2476
Fax: 0171 247 3941
Contracts in account handling, broking and a wide variety of other roles.

MW Appointments
Ibex House
Minories
London
EC3N 1HJ
Tel: 0171 265 1153
Fax: 0171 265 1640
Insurance and reinsurance recruitment specialists with both temporary and contract posts.

Old Broad Street Bureau
65 London Wall
London
EC2M 5TU
Tel: 0171 588 3991
Fax: 0171 588 9012
Always require experienced contractors in: FX, back-up, Eurobond, settlements, documentary credits, off balance sheet etc.

Pertemps City Network
Plantation House
23 Rood Lane
Fenchurch Street
London
EC3M 3DX
Tel: 0171 621 1304
Fax: 0171 626 6671
PC-based contracts.

Prime
Bell Court House
11 Blomfield Street
London
EC2
Tel: 0171 628 3553
Interested in loan administration, accounts, banking and derivatives contractors.

Reed Insurance
24 Lime Street
London
EC3
Tel: 0171 621 0733
Long- and short-term assignments across all disciplines.

Shepherd Little
Cleary Court
21/23 St Swithin's Lane
London
EC4N 8AD
Tel: 0171 626 1161
Fax: 0171 626 9400
Advertises positions such as position keeper, swaps administration, dividend clerks, FX and MM settlements.

Health Service Management

(See also *Executives – Interim Management*)

Contract work in the NHS expanded most rapidly three years ago, when the NHS Trusts were set up. The non-medical professional roles filled by contractors are often project management roles. It can take some time to replace the Director of an NHS Trust, for instance, and it may be necessary to employ a contract Director until the appointment can be made.

Specialized skills, such as contract finance operations management or IT, may be filled by contractors for the same reasons as in other sectors – there are skills shortages and it is sometimes more satisfactory to hire a contractor with exactly the right specialized skills than a permanent employee with more general skills. In the NHS, executive contractors are often known as 'interim managers'.

What kind of contractors fill these roles in the health and related services? According to Judith Hatch, Managing Director of Capita, many of the contractors are career professionals who have taken early retirement or who are between jobs. One of the pluses, as far as the contractors are concerned, is that they can get extra experience by contract-working, since they will work for a greater variety of employers.

For these contractors, the contract premium – the extra pay you can expect as a contractor – is about 50%, so contractors' salaries would be roughly half as much again as the salaries of permanent employees.

Judith Hatch prefers contractors to trade as limited companies, feeling that it is 'more straightforward' than Schedule D. However, Capita also has contractors on PAYE – to some extent it depends on the length of the contract.

Reasons given by other agents in this sector for the growth in contract work included:

- *More flexibility*
  Hiring contract staff is seen as a more flexible way to meet resourcing needs, by calling in expert help as and when you need it.

- *Project-based work*
  As with other organizations, the NHS is seeing a trend towards project-based work, in which a single piece of work can be evaluated and its resourcing requirements evaluated. Psec, another agency operating in this sector emphasized that contractors tended to be mobile, flexible and self-confident – the sort of people who did not need support structures at work and who were capable of producing good quality work, presented in a coherent way.

Different agencies specialize in different areas of the NHS. Some agencies specialize in finance and organizational management, including:

- Costing

- Audit

- Payroll

- Contracts

Other agencies concentrate on areas such as pharmaceuticals or estate management. To find the agency that best fits your skills, you will probably have to ask around and spend some time on the phone, researching possibilities.

Professional consultancy is also growing in the health service, though 'in a controlled way', according to Jean Roberts of GCL (Greenhalgh), who provide consultancy services to the NHS. There are several reasons for this. At the moment there is a fairly fluid market in the NHS as it reorients itself towards dealing with purchasers and providers of health care. Secondly, the Treasury is getting involved in major procurement issues and the procedures are therefore becoming more formalized.

Consultants are therefore being used in a planned way to assist with specific issues. There is certainly a growing market for contractors who are experts in their own fields, whether those be estate management, finance, IT, capital planning or assisting organizations to make effective use of the information they have. However, it is important that these contractors have operational experience.

Greenhalgh often uses multi-disciplinary teams, retaining a small core of specialists and supplementing them as necessary with other experts for specific projects. An average project might last for 50 days, and although they are primarily focused on the health services market they do also undertake projects for vendors such as IT suppliers, because they have independent status and can therefore deliver objective reports.

First Reserve, another agency in this sector, uses contractors who are self-employed, limited companies and PAYE. The range of work they handle can include:

- Final accounts

- Market testing (where the legislation has changed, and the NHS now has to test that it is getting fair value)

- Car leasing

- Interim Financial Directors

First Reserve has definitely noticed a rise in the use of contractors.

As you would expect, agencies in this sector tend to explore contractors' backgrounds thoroughly.

Publications   *Health Service Journal*
Tel: 01256 29242

Agencies   Many agencies have nationwide coverage. To find your nearest office, call the number listed and tell the operator which area you are in.

3 C's
Tel: 01565 652265 or 0171 224 7044
3 C's supply interim management.

Capita
Tel: 0181 560 9997
Fax: 0181 560 9788
Capita supply contract staff to the NHS in these areas: finance, accountancy, general and operations management, business planning, systems, IT, contract-working, market testing.

First Reserve
Phone: 0171 404 6444
First Reserve supply interim management to the Health Services.

Greenhalgh and Company
Tel: 01625 612261
Fax: 01625 511219
Greenhalgh supply management consultancy services to the NHS.

Psec
Tel: 0171 976 7659
Fax: 0171 222 2642
Psec supply interim management across a range of NHS activities.

Information Technology

The market for contract computer professionals is very highly developed. There are more than 300 contract IT agencies, so what follows is a mixed bunch of large and small agencies. Both *Freelance Informer* and *Computer Contractor* carry advertisements from all the main agencies. The British Computer Society now has an Independent Computer Contractors Specialist Group (telephone 01793 417416 for details).

Publications

Freelance Informer
Reed Business Publishing
Subscription Helpline: 01753 567567
Freelance Informer *has a bulletin board service which you can access if you have a modem. The number is 0181 652 3444.*

Computer Contractor
VNU Business Publications
Circulation Hotline: 0171 734 4567

Agencies

Many agencies have nationwide coverage. To find your nearest office, call the number listed and tell the operator which area you are in.

Abraxas
357 Euston Road
London
NW1 3AL
Tel: 0171 388 2061
Fax: 0171 387 3699
Email: contract@abraxas.co.uk
Web site: http//www.abraxas.co.uk/

Answer 42
The Wratten
Wratten Road East
Hitchin
Herts
SG5 2AS
Tel: 01462 422442
Fax: 01462 455442

Arebus
Westmead house
123 Westmead Road
Sutton
SM1 4JH
Tel: 0181 395 1000
Fax: 0181 395 1002

Arena Resources
Lonsdale House
7–9 Lonsdale Gardens
Tunbridge Wells
Kent
TN1 1NU
Tel: 01892 525 232
Fax: 01892 525 233
Email: 100350.3174@compuserve.com
Web site: http://www.cybernation.co.uk/
  cybercon/arena/

Austen Consultancy
Austen House

1 Upper Street
Fleet
Hampshire
GU13 9PE
Tel: 01252 816634
Fax: 01252 811075
Email: austen@pncl.co.uk

Campbell Martin
Prospect House
Sovereign Street
Leeds
LS1 4BJ
Tel: 01709 570110
Fax: 01709 571433
Email: 101333.1117@compuserve.com

Certes
Arthur House
Roman Way
Coleshill
Warwickshire
B46 1HG
Tel: 01675 467475
Fax: 01675 467314
Email: certes@cix.compulink.co.uk

Compass International Group
MGI House
3 Monson Road
Tunbridge Wells
Kent
TN1 1LS
Tel: 01892 548918
Fax: 01892 549994
Email: 100446.367@compuserve.com

Computer People
Computer People Thames Valley
FREEPOST

8 Britannia Court
The Green
West Drayton
Middlesex
UB7 7PN
Tel: 01895 422588
Fax: 01895420909
Email: 100726.741@compuserve.com

Computer Futures
2 Foubert's Place
Regent Street
London
W1V 2AD
Tel: 0171 446 6666
Fax: 0171 446 0095

Computer 2000
11 Harley Street
London
W1N 1DA
Tel: 0171 636 7584
Fax: 0171 580 3734
Email: ctt@2000group.win-uk.net

Computer Team
Charter House
13–15 Carteret Street
London
SW1H 9DJ
Tel: 0171 799 3081
Fax: 0171 222 2423

Comtex
40–41 Old Bond Street
London
W1X 3AF
Tel: 0171 629 6155
Fax: 0171 629 6047
Email: ccv@comtex.demon.co.uk

Cray
127 Fleet Road
Fleet
Hampshire
GU13 8PD
Tel: 01252 625121
Fax: 01252 617665
Email: swc@fleet.craysys.co.uk

CSS Trident
Orchard Fields
Maylands Avenue
Hemel Hempstead
Herts
HP2 7DF
Tel: 01442 240761
Fax: 01442 235449
Email: kbd@css-trident.co.uk

Dart
20 Norton Folgate
Bishopsgate
London
E1 6DB
Tel: 0171 377 9922
Fax: 0171 377 6744
Email: 100572.3317@compuserve.com

DP Support
30 Gordon Street
Glasgow
G1 3PU
Tel: 0141 248 5577
Fax: 0141248 5570

Eaglecliff
30 Pembroke Road
Sevenoaks
Kent
TN13 1XR

Tel: 01732 464644
Fax: 01732 454543
Email: eaglecliff@easynet.co.uk

Elan
93 Newman Street
London
W1P 4DS
Tel: 0171 830 1300
Fax: 0171 830 1333

Eurolink
69–71 Warnford Court
Throgmorton Street
London
EC2N 2AT
Tel: 0171 256 6421
Fax: 0171 256 6266
Email: eurolink@fastnet.co.uk

Executive Recruitment Services
Boundary Way
Hemel Hempstead
Herts
HP2 7RX
Tel: 01442 231691
Fax: 01442 230063
Email: executive@ershemel.demon.co.uk

F. I. Recruitment
Atlantic House
Imperial Way
Worton Grange
Reading
RG2 0TD
Email: xfirecruit@attmail.com

Formula
7a Milburne Road
Westbourne

Bournemouth
BH4 9HJ
Tel: 01202 752660
Fax: 01202 752665
Email: contracts@formula.demon.co.uk

Frost Berkeley Associates
Epworth House
25 City Road
London
EC1Y 1AA
Tel: 0171 374 0374
Fax: 0171 374 4123
Email: lesley@frostb.demon.co.uk
Web site: http://www.jobserve.com/frost-berkeley/

Gatton
Gatton Place
St Matthews Road
Redhill
Surrey
RH1 1TA
Tel: 01737 774100
Fax: 01737 772949
Email: gatton@cix.compulink.co.uk

Harvey Consultants
7 St Paul's Square
Burton on Trent
Staffs
DE14 2EF
Tel: 01283 668093
Fax: 01283 516550
Email: 100345.1077@compuserve.com

Harvey Nash plc
Alice Walsh
Contracts Division
Harvey Nash plc
13 Bruton Street

London
W1X 7AH
Tel: 0171 333 0033
Fax: 0171 333 0032
Email: 100613.1406@compuserve.com

Hayden Pearse Group
61 Cheapside
London
EC2V 6BU
Tel: 0171 236 0151
Fax: 0171 236 2888

Intertech
British National House
Harlands Road
Haywards Heath
West Sussex RH16 1TD
Tel: 01444 450405
Fax: 01444 457112
Email: mail@intertech-grp.co.uk

J. M. Contracts
Chandos House
12–14 Berry Street
London
EC1 0AQ
Tel: 0171 253 7172
Fax: 0171 253 0420

James Duncan and Associates
Seabridge House
8 St John's Road
Tunbridge Wells
Kent
TN4 9NP
Tel: 01892 544757
Fax: 01892 547273
Email: 100432.2211@compuserve.com

JCC
Moorland House
Clitheroe Road
Whalley
Lancs
BB7 9AH
Tel: 01254 824300
Fax: 01254 824730
Email: 100660.1052@compuserve.com

JDF
Marine House
Popham Street
Nottingham
NG1 7JD
Tel: 0115 958 2829
Fax: 0115 950 5440

Kudos
10 Westminster Court
Hipley Street
Woking
Surrey
GU22 9LQ
Tel: 01483 747227
Fax: 01483 747337
Email: 100666.2312@compuserve.com
Web site: http://www.kudos.co.uk/

Macleod Group
11–15 High Street
Marlow
Bucks
SL7 1AU
Tel: 01628 890313
Fax: 01628 890198
Email: macleod@macleodg.demon.co.uk

Modus International
The Tythe Barn

High Street
Edlesborough
Dunstable
Beds
LU6 2HS
Tel: 01525 222222
Fax: 01525 222466
Email: contact@modus.demon.co.uk

Montreal Associates
City Gate House
399–425 Eastern Avenue
Gants Hill
Essex
IG2 6LR
Tel: 0181 518 2211
Fax: 0181 518 3898

Myriad
30 Fleet Street
London
EC4Y 1AA
Tel: 0171 583 2110
Fax: 0171 353 5868
Email: cv@myriad.co.uk

Nesco
Nesco House
98 Weaver Street
Winsford
Cheshire
CW7 4AE
Tel: 01606 550163
Fax: 01606 593739
Email: post@nesco.demon.co.uk

Oldham and Tomkins
3 High Street
Windsor
Berkshire

SL4 1LD
Tel: 01753 850007
Fax: 01753 857449
Email: oldham.tomkins@dial.pipex.com

Oracle Resources Ltd
Oracle Centre
The Ring
Bracknell
Berkshire
RG12 1BW
Tel: 01344 828122
Fax: 01344 828125
Email: Contract.resources@Uk.Oracle.com

Paragon Recruitment
The Business Design Centre
52 Upper Street
London
N1 0QH
Tel: 0171 288 6247
Fax: 0171 288 6248
Email: paragon.rec@dial.pipex.com

PC People
1 St Colme Street
Edinburgh
EH3 6AA
Tel: 0131 220 8262
Fax: 0131 220 3448
Job line: 0171 971 0454
Teletext: Page 641
Web site: http//www.comms.com/

Progressive Computer Recruitment
Contract Service Division
Europa House
266–276 Upper Richmond Road
London
SW15 6TQ

Tel: 0181 785 3333
Fax: 0181 780 0207

Project Management Recruitment
6–8 Broadway
Bexleyheath
Kent
DA6 7LE
Tel: 0181 298 9000
Fax: 0181 298 9988

Real-Time Consultants
118–120 Warwick Street
Royal Leamington Spa
Warwickshire
CV32 4QY
Tel: 01926 313133
Fax: 01926 422165
Email: contract@rtc.co.uk

Rimpac
The Atrium Court
Apex Plaza
Reading
Berks
RG1 1AX
Tel: 01734 254225
Fax: 01734 576626
Email: 100656.2347@.com

Selected Options
South Bank Technopark
90 London Road
London
SE1 6LN
Tel: 0171 922 8818
Fax: 0171 922 8838
Email: 100442.1731@compuserve.com

Software Personnel
FREEPOST ALM 1096
Altrincham
WA15 8BR
Tel: 0161 941 6242
Fax: 0161928 6083
Email: contracts@softwarepsnl.co.uk
Web site: http://www.jobserve.com/sp/

Software Testing People
Kinetic Centre
Theobald Road
Borehamwood
Herts
WD6 4SE
Tel: 0181 236 0258
Fax: 0181953 1118
Email: 100126.2215@compuserve.com

Span
London Office
Piccadilly House
33 Regent Street
London
W1Y 4NB
Tel: 0171 734 7394
Fax: 0171 734 8756
Email: 100441.1607@compuserve.com
Web site: http//www.demon.co.uk/cyberdyne/
   span/span.htm

Square One Resources
154 Bishopsgate
London
EC2M 4LN
Tel: 0171 426 0110
Fax: 0171 426 0111

Tangent
Shelduck House

10 Woodbrook Crescent
Billericay
Essex
CM12 0EQ
Tel: 01277 630055
Fax: 01277 633133
Email: gbtanint@ibmmail.com

TLP
Robert Denholm House
Bletchingley Road
Nutfield
Surrey
RH1 4HW
Tel: 01737 824000
Fax: 01737 824001
Email: bjones@tlplc.com
Web site: http://www.tlpplc.co.uk/

Law

Like doctors, temporary lawyers used to be dignified by the title of 'locums'. But there has been such a huge growth in the use of temporary lawyers that a more belt and braces language is taking over. While I was working a contract at an oil company last year, I met an Australian woman who immediately identified herself as a 'contract lawyer'. In fact since she was working on commercial contracts she was strictly speaking a 'contract contract lawyer'.

Alison Smith at Badenoch and Clark, one of the leading suppliers of contract lawyers, reports that the contract market in this sector is definitely growing, reflecting a general tendency for firms across all sectors to use more contract staff. She describes law firms as something like the planet Jupiter – a set of core permanent people at the centre, surrounded by a ring of contractors on longer-term two- or three-year assignments with an outer ring of shorter term contractors brought in to resource specific projects.

Like so many other recruitment consultants I spoke to, she emphasized flexibility as the key to the contract market. One of the clients' main reasons for using contractors is that it is a very flexible way of filling personnel requirements. But contractors must themselves be prepared to be flexible.

In the legal market there has been some reluctance to take on permanent staff, and another reason for using contractors is that it is a good way of trying people out and seeing whether they would make good permanent employees. For the employers, it cuts down the risks of taking on a new 'unknown quantity' as a permanent employee.

CCT, another agency in the field, quoted a list of reasons why firms might want to employ contractors; these included:

- Maternity leave cover.

- Long-term sickness cover.

- Departmental restructuring.

- Project deadlines to be met in a context where increasing permanent headcount is not allowed; clients are more and more deadline-oriented and this can lead to pressure to employ contractors.

As for contract lawyers – what's in it for them? Well, many of them have tried contract work and found they liked it – my personal guess would be that like other contract workers, they are probably relieved not to have to deal with office politics. Some of them have weathered the recession in permanent jobs they were not particularly enjoying and now feel confident enough about the prospects to leave their permanent jobs and try their hand at contract-working.

Agencies used by lawyers seem to pay them in a variety of ways – some are PAYE and hourly paid; others are self-employed; and some trade as limited companies. Given that lawyers are highly paid, trading as a limited company would seem the most financially attractive option, since it limits the amount of National Insurance that the contractor has to pay.

CCT got special clearance from the Law Society to set up a payroll for lawyers. Since there are fairly high hidden costs for the agency in administering the payroll and taxation aspects of the contractors' pay, it makes sense to do this for a large number of contract lawyers so that the agency can make some economies of scale.

One of the recruitment consultants in the legal profession commented that some lawyers were still scared to leave permanent jobs, even though they expressed a preference for contract-working. But as this consultant said – what *is* job security? It's all in the mind. The same consultant admitted that the major drawback for contractors was difficulty in obtaining mortgages. Come on, building societies: if contract lawyers are not good enough for you, just who *are* you interested in lending to?

Publications
The Lawyer
FREEPOST 39
50 Poland Street
London
W1V 4AX
Tel: 0171 439 4222
Fax: 0171 439 0110

The In-House Lawyer
Tel: 0171 396 9292

Agencies
Many agencies have nationwide coverage. To find your nearest office, call the number listed and tell the operator which area you are in.

ASA Law
Glade House
52 Carter Lane

London
EC4V 5EA
Tel: 0171 236 4625
Nationwide locum specialists.

Badenoch and Clark
16–18 New Bridge Street
London
EC4V 6AU
Tel: 0171 583 0073
Fax: 0171 353 3908
Leading suppliers of contract lawyers

Librarians and Archivists

Masterlock is an agency with activities in several fields, including education. It also has a division which supplies contract librarians and archivists. Most of the work is with large companies, such as large legal firms.

Agencies   Masterlock
Macmillan House
96 Kensington High Street
London
W8 4SG
Tel: 0171 938 1718

Media, Multimedia, Research and Design

Media, design and research are all areas in which the old 'freelance' ethos flourished. What is probably more recent is the growth of agencies in these areas, with the exception of the mainstream media – print and broadcasting. Many broadcasting companies use rolling two- to three-year contracts. This type of arrangement is given a wide berth by contractors in other industries – it has none of the advantages of contract work and all the disadvantages of permanent work.

But in the media you have a strong example of the labour market economy at work: at the lower levels, supply of labour far exceeds demand for it, with a consequent squeeze on pay and conditions. There *are* skills shortages in broadcasting, as in every other industry, and at the time of writing studio directors are in very short supply. However, acquiring these skills is going to involve rather more of the difficult bits than is met with in the average media studies course. Designers good at electronics and IT people who do multimedia are frequently in demand. Researchers tend to be on PAYE contracts because the Inland Revenue has made it clear that it does not consider researchers on contract to be freelances.

There is one agency for researchers – The Research Register. Otherwise, the industry's talent register is *The Blue Book*. Look in *Broadcast* for details.

Like other companies, broadcasting organizations are now moving towards the 'Jupiter' model described by one of the law agencies – an inner core of permies, a ring of people on rolling two- to three-year contracts and an outer circle of freelances.

In addition, the production houses stand in as temporary 'agencies' for the duration of a project, sourcing people and paying them from the budget they have for the programme. For this reason, there are no big agencies in the media, but given how easy and cheap an agency is to set up – you only need contacts, a database and a telephone after all – it is hard to believe that they won't start to appear, at least in the lower levels of the industry.

As far as designers are concerned, I spoke to Mac Recruitment, who explained the seasonal variations in demand for Mac people. They tend to be busiest during the summer period, when holidays need to be covered, and in the Christmas period, when a lot of sales literature, including travel brochures for the following summer, is being prepared.

Their contractors are a mixture of Schedule D sole traders, many of them VAT registered, and PAYE contractors. The PAYE contractors tend to be those who are contracting while they are between jobs, and they are paid fortnightly. Mac Recruitment likes to interview contractors, because CVs can vary so much. Like most agencies, they operate a database and match requirements against contractors' skills.

Publications   *Design Weekly*
Tel: 0171 439 4222

Broadcast
Tel. 01732 770823

Creative Review
Tel: 0171 439 4222

Agencies   Many agencies have nationwide coverage. To find your nearest office, call the number listed and tell the operator which area you are in.

Artworks
114 St Martin's Lane
London
WC2N 4AZ
Tel: 0171 240 9102
Fax: 0171 379 6056
Artworks supplies computer artworkers, graphic designers, product designers, packaging designers, copywriters, art directors and creative directors. It is a division of Kelly, the large recruitment organization.

Artline
Tel: 01920 468017
Fax: 01920 466817
'Places professionals with creative expertise and Mac dexterity.'

The Corps Business
146 Buckingham Palace Road
London
SW1W 9TR
Tel: 0171 259 9898
Supplies freelance and contract designers – they also do Apple Macintosh training

Mac Recruitment
1 Twyford Place
Lincoln's Inn
London Road
High Wycombe
Bucks
HP12 3RE
Tel: 01494 455 477
Freelance designers, trainers, sales, Macintosh operators and Macintosh technical support people.

Recruit Media Ltd
20 Colebrooke Row
London
N1 8AP
Tel: 0171 704 1227
Fax: 0171 704 1370
Agency for Mac/PC creatives, graphics and DTP.

The Research Register
Tel: 0171 700 7573
Supplies freelance researchers for the media.

Workstation Solutions
Tel: 0171 371 7161
Fax: 0171 371 7181
'Specialists in Mac creative recruitment.'

Social Work, Community Care and Medical

This sector tends to have more PAYE contractors than others. There is also a trend towards council social services departments setting up contract divisions, which can result in a very poor deal for contractors (although the nature of the contract market tends to be that contractors vote with their feet, making tracks towards the places where they get the best pay).

At its peak, there were about 35 agencies operating in the social work and community care market. There are now approximately 20 which are active – a couple of large ones and three or four medium-sized ones, with the remainder being small agencies.

One of the largest is Social Workline, which has been established for 14 years. It has 15 000 contractors on its database, and each year they place about 2000 in work. At any one time, about 600 contractors are on assignment. Social Workline deals with several levels of staff, from basic grade practitioner social workers to senior practitioners and deputy and senior managers. It is typical of agencies in most sectors in that the recruitment team have all practised as social workers or managers.

The London Borough of Brent has introduced new recruitment standards for social workers which will also be applied to contract social workers supplied by agencies. Mike Boyle, Director of Brent Social Services, has said that, 'the response from agencies has been encouraging... most agencies believe that employers should evaluate practice skills outside of the traditional interviewing methods'. A small group of staff from Elite Medical Services has completed Brent's new assessment and is waiting for their results. Sybil Reynolds of Elite comments 'We are pleased to support the initiative. Elite already carries out extensive background checks on our staff'.

Publications   *Community Care*
Reed Business Publishing
Tel: 0181 652 4861

The *Guardian* (Wednesday)

Agencies   Many agencies have nationwide coverage. To find your nearest office, call the number listed and tell the operator which area you are in.

Agency Cover Limited
Tel: 0181 808 3339
Takes time to register and is 'very selective'.

ASA Locum Service
The Charter House
Charter Mews
18a Beehive Lane
Ilford
Essex
IG1 3RD

Tel: 0181 544 2111
Places social workers, occupational therapists,
physiotherapists, and speech and language therapists.

BBT
14 Buckingham Palace Road
London
SW1W 0QP
Tel: 0171 233 8999
Fax: 0171 233 8004/5
Deals with Local authorities, education authorities,
NHS trusts and private agencies. Offers free tax advice.

Cooper Stanley Care Services
13 Regent Street
London
SW1Y 4LR
Tel: 0171 976 1999
Deals with newly qualified to senior management
positions.

Elite Medical Services
4–6 Bury Street
St James's
London
SW1Y 6AB
Tel: 0171 839 5000
Fax: 0171 925 2611/2
Specialists in placing social workers, physiotherapists,
occupational therapists, speech/language therapists,
audiologists, pharmacists, MLSOs, radiographers,
hospital doctors and general practitioners.

Principal Care Locums
Tel: 0181 252 5720 (Field)
Tel: 0181 252 5730 (Residential)
Deals with newly qualified to senior management
positions and is open seven days a week.

REED ... care
Tel: 0171 439 0657
Specializes in social work contracts.

Resource Care Services
Tel: 0171 700 0212
Places team managers, residential managers, senior practitioners and children and family workers.

Social Workline
Tel: 0171 383 3939
Social Workline is the largest specialist field and residential agency in the country.

Technical Authors and Translators

Contract technical authors can find themselves writing anything, from highly illustrated books explaining to bar staff how to use the till, to health and safety procedures or complex computer manuals. There are three main specialist agencies for technical writers and one of these also deals with translation.

Paul Morris, recruitment consultant at Kudos, commented on the changes occurring in these professions.

> Writers need to be prepared to see themselves as a business and to invest in that business by acquiring the supplementary skills that are in demand at the moment. For example, at the moment demand exceeds supply for those writers who know how to format written material as on-line help for computer software packages. Whereas for those with traditional skills in preparing written material on paper, supply exceeds demand.

And in the contract market, we all know what that means in terms of rates for the job.

Most of the writers who are registered with Kudos trade as limited companies, but they do have some Schedule D contractors – be prepared to show your Schedule D certificate if you want to trade in this way. Kudos pays writers monthly by BACS, ten days after receiving the invoice.

Publications   *The Author*
Tel: 0171 499 4204

Agencies   Kudos
10 Westminster Court
Hipley Street
Woking
Surrey
GU22 9LQ
Tel: 01483 747227
Fax: 01483 747337
Email: 100666.2312@compuserve.com
Web site: http://www.kudos.co.uk/vacancies/
  Vac-Jobind.html/
(This will take you straight to the page which has
technical writing vacancies listed.)
Kudos supplies contract technical and commercial
authors and translators.

TMS
Hambledon House
Catteshall Lane
Godalming
Surrey
Tel: 01483 414145
TMS supplies contract technical and commercial writers.

Digitext
High Street
Thame
OXON
Tel: 01844 214690
Digitext supplies technical writers.

PART 5 Feedback

Contractor's comment form

Contractors will not be individually identified in any quotations in the *Yearbook* unless they specifically give permission by ticking the box on the form. However, please give a contact address and number, because if you have something to say that is of interest to other contractors, we may contact you and ask for more details.

Please complete the form and send it by fax or post to:

The Publisher, Trade and Professional
McGraw-Hill Publishing Company
Shoppenhangers Road
Maidenhead
Berkshire
SL6 2QL

Tel. 01628 23432
Fax. 01628 770224

Contractor's Comment Form

Name _

Address _
_ _
_ _
_ _
_ _

Tel. _

What kind of work do you do? _ _ _ _ _ _ _ _ _ _ _ _ _ _ _ _ _ _ _
_ _

Do you usually work as a contractor? _ _ _ _ _ _ _ _ _ _ _ _ _ _ _ _

How long have you been a contractor? _ _ _ _ _ _ _ _ _ _ _ _ _ _ _ _

Are there any extra items you would like to see in this Yearbook?
_ _
_ _

Do you use any of these services/policies?

❑ Accountant

❑ Health insurance

❑ Accident insurance

❑ Professional indemnity
   insurance

❑ Employer's liability insurance

❑ Business equipment insurance

❑ Independent financial advice

❑ Private pension

❑ Business bank account

❑ Email service

❑ PC and software

❑ Hotels, bed and breakfasts

What comments would you like to make? Feel free to add an extra page if there is not enough space below.

Agency Request for Free Listing in the 1997 Yearbook

Please complete the form on the following pages and post or fax it to:

The Publisher, Trade and Professional
McGraw-Hill Publishing Company
Shoppenhangers Road
Maidenhead
Berkshire
SL6 2QL

Tel. 01628 23432
Fax. 01628 770224

Agency Listing Request

About the agency

Agency name _

Address _

Tel. _ _ _ _ _ _ _ _ _ _ _ _ Email _ _ _ _ _ _ _ _ _ _ _ _

Fax. _ _ _ _ _ _ _ _ _ _ _ _ Web site URL _ _ _ _ _ _ _ _ _

_ _ _ _ _ _ _ _ _ _ _ _ _ _ _

Contact name: _

As well as a free listing, do you also want to advertise in next year's
Yearbook? _

What areas of work does the agency cover?

_ _

_ _

_ _

_ _

_ _

Does the agency have nationwide coverage?

_ _

Does the agency have European coverage?

_ _

How long is a typical contract assignment?

_ _

Is the agency a member of FRES or any other professional association?

_ _

How long has the agency been established and what was its turnover last
year? _

_ _

_ _

How many contractors do you have on your database?

_ _

Paying contract staff

How do people working on contract for you trade? Tick the categories which apply.

❏ Self-employed Schedule D   ❏ Umbrella companies

❏ Limited companies   ❏ PAYE

How often do you pay contract staff? _

What method of payment do you use? _

How many days after receiving a contractor's invoice, do you pay? _

Do you have any special deals, services or benefits for contractors? _

How do you prefer contractors to make the initial approach (posted CV, phone call, email etc.)? _

Any other comments you would like to make about contract work in your sector:

Index